My No-Knead

Turbo Bread Cookbook

Introducing "Hands-Free" Technique

From the kitchen of
Artisan Bread with Steve

Updated 6.12.2016

By
Steve Gamelin

Copyright © 2014 by Steve Gamelin

All rights reserved. No part of this book may be used or reproduced, stored in a retrieval system, or transmitted in an form or by an means—electronics, mechanical, or any other—except for brief quotations in print reviews without prior permission of the author.

Now that I have met the standard legal requirements I would like to give my personal exceptions. I understand this is a cookbook and anyone who purchases this book can, (a) print and share the recipes with their friends, as you do with your other cookbooks (of course, it is my hope they too will start to make no-knead bread and buy my cookbooks) and (b) you may share a recipe or two on your website, etc. as long as you note the source and provide instructions on how your audience can acquire this book.

Thanks – Steve

Table of Contents

"Table of Contents" lists both recipe and method (bakeware) used to shape and bake loaf, but you can mix and match... the ingredients from one recipe with the method (bakeware) from a different recipe. The two components are independent of each other. For example, you can use the ingredients from the "Harvest 8 Grain Whole Wheat Bread (long covered baker)" recipe... proof for 1-1/2 hours... then use the method (bakeware) from the "Country White Bread (standard bread pan)" recipe. In other words... you can bake harvest 8 grain whole wheat bread in a standard bread pan by following the country white recipe's standard bread pan method. Any recipe... any method (bakeware).

Quick Note from Steve 1

The Two Basic Methods for Making No-Knead Bread 2

Ingredients 4

    Flour 4

    Salt 4

    Yeast 5

    Water 5

    Other Ingredients 6

    Flavor Ingredients 6

Technique & Tips 7

    Prep 7

    Combining Ingredients 7

    1st Proofing (dynamics of proofing) 7

    Degas, Pull & Stretch 9

    Roll to Coat 9

    Garnish & Baste (optional) 9

    Divide & Shape 9

    2nd Proofing 10

Score (optional)	10
Bake	10
Storing Dough (refrigerate | freeze | thaw)	11
Equipment & Bakeware	11
Bread	**13**
Country White Bread (standard bread pan)	14
Skillet Bread (skillet)	16
Sandwich Bread (poor man's Dutch oven)	18
American Baguettes (baguette pan)	20
Beer Bread (mini round baker – half loaves)	22
Cheddar Cheese Bread (preheated Dutch oven)	24
Multigrain Country White Bread (standard bread pan)	26
Italian Sesame Sandwich Bread (poor man's Dutch oven)	28
Italian Sesame Boule (preheated Dutch oven)	30
Muffuletta - Sicilian Sesame Bread (9" pie pan)	32
Honey Oatmeal Bread (uncovered baker)	34
Honey Whole Wheat Bread (preheated Dutch oven)	36
Harvest 8 Grain Whole Wheat Bread (long covered baker)	38
Flax Seed 8 Grain Bread (standard bread pan)	40
Rosemary Bread (mini round baker – half loaves)	42
Caraway Rye Bread (standard bread pan)	44
Polenta Bread (preheated uncovered baker)	46
Mediterranean Olive Bread (long loaf pan – half loaves)	48
Mexican Jalapeño-Chili Fiesta Bread (preheated uncovered baker)	50

Buttermilk Bread (long covered baker) 52

Cinnamon Raisin Bread (small bread pan) 54

English Muffin Loaf (small bread pan) 56

Rolls & Buns 59

Traditional Dinner Rolls (jumbo muffin pans) 60

Pull-Apart Dinner Rolls (pull-apart - baste) 62

Garlic-Cheese Rolls (muffin cutter) 64

Multigrain Country White Rolls (hand shaped) 66

Garlic-Herb Rolls (mini round cake pans) 68

Honey Whole Wheat Rolls (mini round cake pans) 70

Harvest 8 Grain Whole Wheat Rolls (baguette pans) 72

Mediterranean Olive Signature Rolls (mini round cake pans) 74

Cinnamon Raisin Breakfast Rolls (mini round cake pans) 76

Small Sandwich Rolls (mini loaf pans) 78

Large Sandwich Rolls (baguette pans) 80

Torpedo Sandwich Rolls (baguette pans) 82

Hamburger Buns (mini round cake pans) 84

No-Knead Pizza Dough & Pizza 86

No-Knead Pizza Dough 87

"Traditional" No-Knead Pizza Dough… proof for 8 to 24 hours 88

No-Knead "Turbo" Pizza Dough… proof for 1-1/2 hours 89

Mushroom-Black Olive Pizza 90

Pepperoni Pizza 91

Whole Wheat Cheese Pizza 92

- Meatball & Bacon Pizza 93
- Garlic Breadsticks & Nuggets 94

Sweet Rolls 95

- No-Knead "Turbo" Sweet Roll Dough 96
- Old-Fashioned Cinnamon Rolls (Pan Method) 98
- Old-Fashioned Cinnamon Rolls (Individual Roll Method) 100
- Raspberry Sweet Rolls 102
- Almond Danish 104
- Caramel-Pecan Sweet Rolls (a.k.a. Sticky Buns) 106

Quick Note from Steve

Hi... I'm Steve, my YouTube channel is "ArtisanBreadWithSteve" on which I have a selection of educational videos demonstrating no-knead bread recipes and technique. Over the years I have worked with my readers and subscribers listening to their desires and needs... to have high quality, great tasting, fresh from the oven bread that is fast, convenient, hassle-free, and reliable without special equipment or expensive bakeware. In response, I developed no-knead "Turbo" bread (ready to bake in 2-1/2 hours), "hands-free" technique (bread can go straight from mixing bowl to baking vessel without dusting work surface with flour or touching the dough), and "roll to coat" (coat dough with flour in mixing bowl... no more sticky dough).

Now, don't get me wrong... I love the "traditional" method of making no-knead bread, but there are times when I need bread in less time and I can have no-knead "Turbo" bread ready for the oven in less than 2-1/2 hours... without touching the dough!

No-knead "Turbo" bread, "hands-free" technique, and "roll to coat" are fresh approaches to making no-knead bread that provides you with an option. Try it... you'll love it.

Thanks - Steve

The Two Basic Methods for Making No-Knead Bread

There are two basic methods… traditional and turbo.

"Traditional" No-Knead Method
The traditional no knead method uses long proofing times (8 to 12 hours) to develop flavor and was designed to be baked in a Dutch oven. The purpose of the Dutch oven is to emulate a baker's oven by trapping the moisture from the dough in a "screaming" hot, enclosed environment. This is an excellent method for making artisan quality bread.

Recommended YouTube video: World's Easiest No-Knead Bread (Introducing "Hands-Free" Technique)

No-Knead "Turbo" Method
The no-knead "Turbo Method" uses shorter proofing times (ready to bake in 2-1/2 hours) and was designed to be baked in traditional bakeware (bread pan, etc.). It was designed for those who want to make no-knead bread, but… don't want to wait 8 to 24 hours. Those who want bread machine bread, but… don't want to buy and store a bread machine. It's for those of you who want a fast reliable way to make fresh from the oven bread without the hustle of expensive machines, Dutch ovens, or kneading.

Recommended YouTube video: Ultimate Introduction to No-Knead "Turbo" Bread… ready to bake in 2-1/2 hours

This cookbook uses the "Turbo" method of making no-knead bread.

Advantages of No-Knead "Turbo" Bread, Rolls, & Pizza are…

(1) Shorter time… bread is ready to bake in less than 2-1/2 hours.

(2) No kneading… Mother Nature does the kneading for you.

(3) No yeast proofing… instant yeast doesn't require proofing.

(4) No special equipment (no mixer, no bread machine) the entire process is done in a glass bowl with a spoon and a spatula… and can be baked in a wide variety of baking vessels (standard bread pan, uncovered baker, skillet, preheated Dutch oven, etc.).

(5) Only uses 4 basic ingredients (flour, salt, yeast and water) to which other ingredients can be added to make a variety of specialty breads.

(6) "Hands-free" technique uses the handle end of a plastic spoon to manipulate the dough (like a dough hook) which allows the dough to go

straight from the mixing bowl to the baking vessel (bread pan, etc.) without dusting the work surface with flour or touching the dough.

(7) And "roll to coat"… an innovative process that coats the dough ball with flour… in the mixing bowl… no more sticky dough. When the dough comes out of the bowl it will be easy to handle if you wish to divide the dough into portion to make baguettes, rolls, etc.

Some have said, no-knead "Turbo" bread is bread machine bread… without the bread machine. I like to think of it as a way for the average family to have fresh from the oven bread in the convenience of their homes without special equipment or any hassles.

Ingredients

It only takes four ingredients to make bread... flour, salt, yeast and water.

Flour
Flour is the base ingredient of bread and there are four basic types of flour...

(1) Bread flour is designed for yeast bread. It has a higher percentage of gluten which gives artisan bread its airy crumb.

(2) All-purpose flour has less gluten than bread flour. I use all-purpose flour for biscuits, flatbreads, etc. In other words... I use it when I don't want an airy crumb.

(3) Self-rising flour is all-purpose flour with baking soda and baking powder added as leavening agents. It's intended for quick breads... premixed and ready to go. Do not use self-rising flour to make yeast bread. To see the difference between yeast and quick breads you may want to watch Introduction to No-Knead Beer Bread (a.k.a. Artisan Yeast Beer Bread) and Introduction to Quick Beer Bread (a.k.a. Beer Bread Dinner Rolls).

(4) And there are a variety of specialty flours... whole wheat, rye, and a host of others. Each has its unique flavor and characteristics. In some cases, you can substitute specialty flour for bread flour, but you may need to tweak the recipe because most specialty flours have less gluten. I frequently blend specialty flour with bread flour.

Flour is the primary ingredient... if you don't use the correct flour you won't get the desired results.

Note: To know how many cups of flour there are in a specific bag... it's typically on the side in "Nutritional Facts". For example, this bag reads, "Serving Size 1/4 cup... Serving Per Container about 75". In other words... 18.75 (75 times 1/4). That's the technical answer, but in the real world (measuring cup versus weight) a bag of flour will measure differently based on density (sifted versus unsifted), type of flour (wheat is more dense than bread flour), humidity (flour weighs more on humid days), and all the other variables life and nature have to offer. There is no single correct answer, but for practical purposes... figure a 5# bag of bread flour is 17 to 18 cups.

Salt
While it is possible to make bread without salt... you would be disappointed. There are three basics types of salt...

(1) Most baking recipes are designed to use everyday table salt unless specified otherwise. Unless you're experienced, it is probably smartest to use table salt for your baking needs.

(2) <u>Kosher salt</u> is excellent. I use it when I cook, but a tablespoon of kosher salt does not equal a tablespoon of table salt because kosher salt crystals are larger.

(3) And, I use <u>specialty salt</u> as a garnish... for appearance and taste. For example, I use sea salt to garnish pretzels.

Generally speaking, when salt is added as an ingredient and baked it is difficult to taste the difference between table, kosher and sea salt. When salt is added as a garnish and comes in contact with the taste buds... kosher or specialty salt is an excellent choice.

Yeast

Yeast is the "magic" ingredient which transforms flour and water into dough. My traditional no-knead recipes use 1/4 tsp yeast… I want the dough to rise slowly which allows the dough to develop flavor. My "Turbo" recipes use 1-1/4 tsp yeast… I want a faster rises like traditional bread recipes. There are three basic types of yeast...

(1) The most common is <u>active dry yeast</u> which needs to be proof in warm water prior to being added to flour.

(2) I use <u>instant dry yeast</u> (a.k.a. "instant yeast", "bread machine yeast", "quick rise", "rapid rise", "fast rising", etc.) which does not need to be proofed in warm water. It is a more recent development which is more potent and reliable... and why worry about proofing yeast if you don't have too.

(3) Some older recipes call for <u>cake yeast</u> (a.k.a. "compressed yeast" or "fresh yeast"), but it's perishable. Most bakers substitute active and instant dry yeast for cake yeast when using older recipes.

The names on the bottles can be confusing. When in doubt, read the instructions and look for one that does not require soaking the yeast in warm water prior to use.

Water

Water hydrates the ingredients and activates the yeast. The no-knead method uses a little more water than the typical recipe... and that's a good thing. It makes it easier to combine the wet and dry ingredients, and contributes to its airy crumb.

(1) I use <u>warm Water</u>. It's convenient and easy, but sometimes city water has too much chlorine (chlorine kills yeast).

(2) If your dough does not rise during first proofing you may want to use <u>bottled drinking water</u>.

(3) But, do not use <u>distilled water</u> because the minerals have been removed.

Water is a flavor ingredient, if your water doesn't taste good... use bottled drinking water.

Other Ingredients
Some recipes will include sugar, eggs, milk, vegetable oil, shortening, and a variety of other ingredients... each has its purpose, but I prefer the basics (flour, salt, yeast and water) because it gives me bakery quality artisan bread with a beautiful airy crumb... you'll love the flavor.

Flavor Ingredients
It only takes four ingredients to make bread... flour, salt, yeast and water, to which a variety of flavor ingredients can be added to make specialty breads such as... honey whole wheat, multi-grain white, rosemary, Mediterranean olive, cinnamon raisin, honey oatmeal, and a host of others.

Technique & Tips

The technique discussed in this section is demonstrated on YouTube in <u>Ultimate Introduction to No-Knead "Turbo" Bread… ready to bake in 2-1/2 hours</u>.

Prep
To insure consistency and assist Mother Nature with the task of kneading the dough for you… it's important to provide yeast with a warm environment. One of the keys to proofing temperature is the temperature of the mixing bowl because it has direct contact with the dough while proofing. So… it is important to use a warm bowl.

Combining Ingredients
Pour warm water in a 3 to 4 qt warm glass mixing bowl (use a warm bowl… you don't want a cold bowl to take the heat out of the warm water). Add salt, yeast, flavor ingredients, etc… and stir to combine (it will insure the ingredients are evenly distributed). Add flour (flour will resist the water and float). Start by stirring the ingredients with the handle end of a plastic spoon drawing the flour from the sides into the middle of bowl (vigorously mixing will not hydrate the flour faster… but it will raise a lot of dust). Within 30 seconds the flour will hydrate and form a shaggy ball. Then scrape dry flour from side of bowl and tumble dough to combine moist flour with dry flour (about 15 seconds). It takes about one minute to combine wet and dry ingredients.

Place bowl in a warm draft free location, cover bowl with a lint-free towel, and proof for 1-1/2 hours.

1st Proofing (dynamics of proofing)
The process is called "proofing" because it "proves" your yeast is active. If your dough does <u>not</u> rise the usual culprits are… outdated yeast or chlorinated water (chlorine kills yeast). Solution, get fresh yeast and/or use bottled drinking water.

If your dough is <u>slow</u> (takes "forever") to rise… your proofing temperature is too cool. The best test for temperature is the proofing vessel (mixing bowl) because it is in contact with the dough… it should feel warm to the touch.

Background: Bread making is nature at work (yeast is a living organism) and subject to nature. Seasons (summer vs. winter) and weather (heat & humidity) have a direct impact on proofing. In other words, don't worry if your dough varies in size… that's Mother Nature. Just focus on your goal… if the gluten forms (the dough has a stringy nature) and doubles in size… you're good to go.

The ideal proofing temperature is 78 to 85 degrees F… which is why recipes generally suggest proofing in a "<u>warm</u> draft-free location", but dough can be proofed in a wide range of temperatures and conditions. Our ancestor didn't have heating or air conditioning... they adjusted to nature. They waited until the dough doubled in size which was shorter in summer and longer in winter. Likewise, you can proof at any temperature… if you're will to wait for the dough to double in size, but there are techniques that can stimulate proofing.

Direct sunlight: In winter I like to proof in direct sunlight. The heat from the Sun will create a favorable environment for proofing. And on cloudy days when you don't have direct sunlight there are other options…

Oven setting: If your oven has a proofing temperature (80 degrees F)… use it.

Oven light: If your oven has an oven light… turn the oven light on, place mixing bowl (dough) in the oven and close the door. The light will generate heat and increase the temperature inside the oven by several degrees. The amount of heat will depend on the size of the oven and strength of the bulb. The oven temperature will always start below your thermostat, climb slowly, but may go over 90 degrees F. so check periodically until you are familiar with the nature of your oven.

Microwave proofing: Place an 8 to 16 oz cup of water in the microwave and heat on high for 2 minutes. Then move the cup to the back corner, place mixing bowl (dough) in microwave and close the door. The heat and steam from the hot water will create a favorable environment for proofing.

Preheated oven: When all else fails… set oven to your oven's lowest setting. When it reaches 120 degrees F... turn oven off, put mixing bowl (dough) in oven and leave door 3" to 4" ajar. With the door ajar the oven will cool rapidly. Then, check every 30 minutes. As soon as it has doubled in size… remove it from the oven and finish proofing on the countertop. I generally take the dough out after 60 minutes of oven proofing.

Proofing ovens: Most commercial kitchens have proofing ovens (big metal cabinet with racks for trays of dough) to controls the climate and temperature which gives them consistency. There are smaller versions for the public that fold flat (folding bread proofers) for those of you who also want consistency.

Bottom-line… 90% of the time dough can be proofed on the countertop or in direct sunlight. But on cold days without Sun… you may want to create a warm draft-free environment for proofing or extend the proofing time.

Tip: To fit bread making into your schedule… you can extend 1st proofing up to 4 hours (or even more), but don't shorten… it important to give Mother Nature time to form the gluten.

Supporting video: How to Proof Bread Dough (a.k.a. The Dynamics of Proofing)

Degas, Pull & Stretch

The purpose of degassing, pulling and stretching is to, (a) expel the gases that formed during bulk fermentation, (b) strengthen the dough by realigning and stretching the gluten strands, and (c) stimulate yeast activity for 2nd proofing.

Because no-knead dough is sticky and difficult to handle… I degas, pull & stretch dough by stirring it with the handle end of a plastic spoon in the bowl (like a dough hook). It will reduce the size of the dough ball by 50% making it easier to handle and the process replaces folding and shaping in most cases.

Roll to Coat

Before removing the dough from bowl… dust the dough and side of the bowl with flour, then roll to coat. The flour will bond to the sticky dough making it easier to handle, but do not roll to coat with flour if you're going to "Garnish & Baste".

Garnish & Baste (optional)

The purpose of garnishing and basting is to enhance the appearance of the crust, but it isn't necessary. If you decide to garnish and baste there are two techniques… roll to coat and skillet method.

Roll to Coat Method: Before removing dough from bowl… add ingredients to bowl (on the dough and side of the bowl), then roll to coat. For example, when I garnish honey oatmeal bread… I sprinkle oat in the bowl and on the dough, then roll the dough ball in the oats and they will bond to the sticky dough. This can also be done with seeds, grains, olive oil, egg wash, etc.

Skillet Method: When I want to garnish and/or baste the top of the loaf… I coat the proofing skillet with baste (egg wash, olive oil, vegetable oil, etc.) and sprinkle with the garnish (oats, seeds, grains, etc.). The ingredients will bond with the dough as the dough proofs.

Supporting video: How to Garnish & Baste No-Knead Bread using "Hands-Free" Technique

Divide & Shape

If you're not going to divide the dough… it can go straight from the mixing bowl to the proofing or baking vessel. If you are going to divide and shape the dough… roll the dough ball out of the bowl (excess flour and all) onto the work surface to divide and shape. Then add flour to the work surface as needed… it will make it easier. I use a plastic bowl scraper to assist in dividing, shaping and transporting the dough to the baking vessel. Together they (flour & bowl scraper) make it easier to handle the dough.

2nd Proofing

Place the proofing or baking vessel in a warm draft-free location and proof for 30 minutes. The dough will expand and conform to the shape of the baking vessel.

To fit bread making into your schedule… you can extend 2nd proofing times, but you don't want the dough to exceed the size of the baking vessel. If you're using a large baking vessel (Dutch oven, etc.) it's never a problem, but if you're using a bread pan your loaf will droop over the sides and be less attractive. But, always bake it… it will still be delicious.

Score (optional)

The purpose of scoring dough is to provide seams to control where the crust will split during "oven spring", but it isn't necessary to score dough. If you do decide to score your loaf you may want to use a scissors (no-knead dough is very moist and more likely to stretch than slice). Personally, I place the dough in the baking vessel seam side up… the dough will split at the seam during "oven spring" which gives the loaf a nice rustic appearance.

Bake

Baking Time: Bread is done when it reaches an internal temperature of 185 to 220 degrees F and the crumb (inside of the bread) isn't doughy. Baking times in my recipes are designed to give bread an internal temperature of 200 to 205 degrees F, but ovens vary and you may need to adjust your baking times slightly.

No-Stick Spray: Most bakeware has a non-stick surface, but it is safest to spray your bakeware unless you are fully confident your bread won't stick.

Ovens: Ovens don't always tell the truth. I check the temperature of ovens and bakeware. Ovens with a digital readout that displays the temperature as they preheat are typically very accurate, but ovens that say they will be at temperature in a specific number of minutes are not always accurate. My point is… you will get the best results if you learn the character and nature of your oven.

Oven Rack: Generally speaking you want to bake bread and rolls in the middle or lower third of the oven, but it isn't critical. Just keep them away from the upper heating element or they may brown a little too quickly.

Oven Spring: When dough is first put into the oven they will increase in size by as much as a third in a matter of minutes because, (a) gases trapped in the dough will expand, (b) moisture will turn into steam and try to push its way out, and (c) yeast will become highly active converting sugars into gases. The steam and gases work together to create "oven spring". Once the internal temperature of the bread reaches 120 degrees F… the yeast will begin to die and the crust will harden.

Storing Dough (refrigerate | freeze | thaw)
If you wish to save dough... divide into portions, drizzle each portion with olive oil, place in zip-lock bag, remove excess air, and refrigerate for up to two days or freeze for up to two months. To thaw dough... move dough from freezer to refrigerator the day before (12 or more hours), then place on counter for 30 minutes before use to come to room temperature.

Equipment & Bakeware
Bowl for Mixing: You can use any 3 to 4 qt bowl. I use a 3-1/2 qt glass bowl because, (a) there's ample room for the dough to expand, (b) plastic wrap sticks to glass, and (c) I don't want the rim of my bowl to exceed the width of the plastic wrap.

Measuring Spoons: I'm sure you already have measuring spoons in the kitchen... they will work just fine. If you're going to buy new, I prefer oval versus round because an oval shape will fit into jars and containers more easily.

Measuring Cups: Dry measuring cups are designed to be filled to the top and leveled. Liquid measuring cups have a pour spout and are designed to be filled to the gradations on the side (neither measures weight). Because of their design and a slight difference in volume, it is best to use the appropriate measuring cup.

Note: U.S. and metric measuring cups may be used interchangeably... there is only a slight difference (±3%). More importantly, the ingredients of a recipe measured with a set (U.S. or metric) will have their volumes in the same proportion to one another.

Spoon for Combining Wet and Dry Ingredients: A spoon is an excellent tool for combining wet and dry ingredients. Surprisingly, I found the handle end of a plastic spoon worked best for me because, I didn't have a big clump on the end like it did with some of my other mixing utensils (which makes it easier to stir and manipulate the dough). And when you think about it... mixers don't use a paddle to mix dough, they use a hook which looks a lot like the handle end of my spoon.

Silicon Baking Mat: Silicone baking mats are very useful... I use them as reusable parchment paper (they're environmentally friendly). Silicone baking mats serve two purposes... (a) as a work surface for folding and shaping (they have excellent non-stick properties), and (b) as a baking mat... specifically when the dough is difficult to move after folding and shaping. And I slide a cookie sheet under the mat before baking (it makes it easier to put the mat into and take it out of the oven).

Spatula: I use a spatula to scrape the sides of the bowl to get the last bits of flour incorporated into the dough.

Plastic Bowl Scraper: I use a plastic bowl scraper verses a metal dough scraper because it's the better multi-tasker. I use the bowl scraper to (a) fold, shape, and divide the dough, (b) assist in transporting the dough it to the proofing vessel, (c) then I use it to scrape the excess flour off the work surface, (d) scrape the excess flour out of the bowl (after all it is a bowl scraper), and (e) scrape any remaining bits in the sink towards the disposal. It's a useful multi-tasker.

Timer: I'm sure you already have a timer in the house. Any that you already have will work just fine. I prefer digital because they're more accurate.

Baking Vessels: Baking vessels come in a variety of sizes, shapes and materials. You can change the appearance of the loaf by sampling changing the baking vessel.

Plastic Wrap & Proofing Towel: When proofing for extended periods of time (8 to 24 hours), I use plastic wrap to protect the dough. Generally speaking, I use plastic wrap when I proof for over 2 hours to protect the dough and a lent-free towel for shorter durations except when proofing in direct sunlight (plastic wrap traps heat from the Sun on cold days). And, any lint-free towel can be used to cover your dough during 1st and 2nd proofing.

Cooling Rack: The purpose of a cooling rack is to expose the bottom of the loaf during the cooling process.

Bread Bags: I use plastic bread bags to store bread after they have cooled. And they're great for packaging bread as gifts. I also use paper bags as gifts when the loaf is still warm and I don't want to trap the moisture in a plastic bag… it gives a nice natural appearance.

Bread

One simple recipe, four ingredients, no kneading, no yeast proofing, no mixer... just a little tweaking and you can create a variety of artisan breads that you would be proud to serve your family and friends.

To further expand your repertoire, these recipes have a dual purpose... ingredients for specific breads and technique (methods) for a variety of baking vessels. The recipes use...

Small bread pan
Standard bread pan
Long loaf pan (half loaves)
Baguette pan
Skillet
Poor man's Dutch oven
Preheated Dutch oven
Uncovered baker
Preheated uncovered baker
Long covered baker
Mini round baker (half loaves)
Pie pan

My point is... you can use the ingredients from one recipe and the technique (method) from another. The options are endless.

Country White Bread (standard bread pan)
Country White is the most popular artisan bread. It's simple... it's basic. And, if you're making your first loaf... this is the place to start.

I used a *Chicago Metallic* bread pan (8-1/2" x 4-1/2") to shape this loaf. The bread pan is the #1 baking vessel for bread (most common), but you can use any anything from a preheated Dutch oven (the traditional no-knead method) to an uncovered baker.

YouTube Video in support of recipe: Introduction to No-Knead Turbo Bread (Ready to Bake in 2-1/2 Hours with Just a Spoon and a Bowl)

Country White Bread

Pour warm water in a 3 to 4 qt warm glass mixing bowl (use a warm bowl… you don't want a cold bowl to take the heat out of the warm water).

    14 oz warm Water

Add salt and yeast… give a quick stir to combine.

    1-1/2 tsp Salt
    1-1/4 tsp Instant Yeast

Add flour… stir until dough forms a shaggy ball, scrape dry flour from side of bowl, then tumble dough to combine moist flour with dry flour.

    3-1/2 cups Bread Flour

Place bowl in a warm draft-free location, cover with a lint-free towel (or plastic wrap), and proof for 1-1/2 hours.

1-1/2 hours later (standard bread pan)

When dough has risen and developed its gluten structure… spray an 8-1/2" x 4-1/2" bread pan with no-stick cooking spray and set aside.

Start by putting handle end of spoon in center of dough and "degas, pull and stretch" dough to form a ball.

Generously dust dough and side of bowl with flour… roll dough in flour to coat. Roll dough out of bowl into bread pan.

Place pan in a warm draft-free location, cover with a lint-free towel, and proof for 30 minutes.

Before dough is fully proofed…

Move rack to middle of oven and pre-heat to 400 degrees F.

30 minutes later

When oven has come to temperature… place bread pan in oven and bake for 40 minutes.

40 minutes later

Gently turn loaf out on work surface and place on cooling rack.

Skillet Bread (skillet)
Simple recipe… simple technique… great results, and I garnished the loaf with sesame seed. It's really very simple. I didn't even have to touch the dough.

I used a *Lodge* cast iron 10-1/2" skillet to shape this loaf, but you can use any 8" to 10-1/2" oven safe skillet (make sure the handle is oven safe). A smaller 8" skillet will constrain the dough during oven bounce and force the dough to expand upwards and give you a tall plump boule, while a larger 10-1/2" skillet will allow the dough to expand outwards filling the skillet and give you a broad low profile boule.

YouTube Video in support of recipe: How to Bake No-Knead "Turbo" Bread in a Skillet (ready to bake in 2-1/2 hours)

Skillet Bread

Pour warm water in a 3 to 4 qt warm glass mixing bowl (use a warm bowl… you don't want a cold bowl to take the heat out of the warm water).

    14 oz warm Water

Add salt and yeast… give a quick stir to combine.

    1-1/2 tsp Salt
    1-1/4 tsp Instant Yeast

Add flour… stir until dough forms a shaggy ball, scrape dry flour from side of bowl, then tumble dough to combine moist flour with dry flour.

    3-1/2 cups Bread Flour

Place bowl in a warm draft-free location, cover with a lint-free towel (or plastic wrap), and proof for 1-1/2 hours.

1-1/2 hours later (skillet - garnish)

When dough has risen and developed its gluten structure… spray skillet with no-stick cooking spray and set aside.

Start by putting handle end of spoon in center of dough and "degas, pull and stretch" dough to form a ball.

Garnish… sprinkle dough and side of bowl with seeds and roll to coat.

    2 Tbsp Sesame Seeds

Generously dust dough and side of bowl with flour… roll dough in flour to coat. Roll dough out of bowl into skillet.

Place skillet in a warm draft-free location, cover with a lint-free towel, and proof for 30 minutes.

Before dough is fully proofed…

Move rack to middle of oven and pre-heat to 400 degrees F.

30 minutes later

When oven has come to temperature… place skillet in oven and bake for 40 minutes.

40 minutes later

Gently turn loaf out on work surface and place on cooling rack.

Sandwich Bread (poor man's Dutch oven)
Want a Dutch oven that will shape sandwich bread… no problem… use a "poor man's Dutch oven". You'll get a kick out of this recipe. It's unconventional, it's silly, but who cares because the technique is so good that it has become our standard for making sandwich bread.

I used two *Good Cook* (8" x 4" x 2-1/4") loaf pans to shape this loaf. I liked the size and the handles made it easy to clip the top to the bottom.

Option: Because of the pans smaller size (4" x 8" vs. 4-1/2" x 8-1/2" or 9" x 5") I used 3 cups flour. If you use a larger size pan… use 14 oz water, 3-1/2 cups flour, 1-1/2 tsp salt, and 1-1/4 tsp yeast and bake for 40 minutes.

YouTube Video in support of recipe: How to Bake No-Knead Bread in a Poor Man's Dutch Oven (no mixer… no bread machine)

Sandwich Bread

Pour warm water in a 3 to 4 qt warm glass mixing bowl (use a warm bowl… you don't want a cold bowl to take the heat out of the warm water).

<u>12 oz warm Water</u>

Add salt and yeast… give a quick stir to combine.

<u>1-1/2 tsp Salt</u>
<u>1 tsp Instant Yeast</u>

Add flour… stir until dough forms a shaggy ball, scrape dry flour from side of bowl, then tumble dough to combine moist flour with dry flour.

<u>3 cups Bread Flour</u>

Place bowl in a warm draft-free location, cover with a lint-free towel (or plastic wrap), and proof for 1-1/2 hours.

1-1/2 hours later (poor man's Dutch oven)

When dough has risen and developed its gluten structure… spray bottom pan with no-stick spray and set aside.

Start by putting handle end of spoon in center of dough and "degas, pull and stretch" dough to form a ball.

Scrape side of bowl to get remaining dough into dough ball.

Generously dust dough and side of bowl with flour, roll dough in flour to coat.

Roll dough out of bowl into bread pan.

Cover bottom bread pan with top pan and place in a warm draft-free location to proof for 30 minutes.

Before dough is fully proofed…

Move rack to lower third of oven and pre-heat to 400 degrees F.

30 minutes later

When oven has come to temperature… place poor man's Dutch oven in the oven and bake for 35 minutes.

35 minutes later

Take pans out of the oven, remove the top, and place pan back in the oven for 3 to 15 minutes to finish the crust.

3 to 15 minutes later

Gently turn loaf out on work surface and place on cooling rack.

American Baguettes (baguette pan)
Baguettes are very popular because of their shape. They're ideally suited for garlic cheese bread, bruschetta, sandwiches, etc.

I used 2 *Matfer* 311141 double loaf French bread pan (18"x 2") because they have a smooth baking surface. Previously I used perforated baguette pans, but I had too much trouble with the dough sticking in the perforations.

YouTube Video in support of recipe: Easy No-Knead "Turbo" Baguettes... ready to bake in 2-1/2 hours

American Baguettes

Pour warm water in a 3 to 4 qt warm glass mixing bowl (use a warm bowl… you don't want a cold bowl to take the heat out of the warm water).

<u>14 oz warm Water</u>

Add salt and yeast… give a quick stir to combine.

<u>1-1/2 tsp Salt</u>
<u>1-1/4 tsp Instant Yeast</u>

Add flour… stir until dough forms a shaggy ball, scrape dry flour from side of bowl, then tumble dough to combine moist flour with dry flour.

<u>3-1/2 cups Bread Flour</u>

Place bowl in a warm draft-free location, cover with a lint-free towel (or plastic wrap), and proof for 1-1/2 hours.

1-1/2 hours later (baguette pan)

When dough has risen and developed its gluten structure… spray baguette pans with no-stick spray and set aside.

Start by putting handle end of spoon in center of dough and "degas, pull and stretch" dough to form a ball.

Generously dust dough and side of bowl with flour… roll dough in flour to coat.

Roll dough (and excess flour) out of bowl onto work surface.

Press lightly to flatten… and divide dough into 3 portions.

Then (one portion at a time) roll dough on work surface in flour to shape and stretch into 14" lengths and place in pan. (When shaping, I find holding the dough over the work surface and allowing gravity to stretch helps with the process.)

Place pans in a warm draft-free location, cover with a lint-free towel, and proof for 30 minutes.

Before dough is fully proofed…

Move rack to middle of oven and pre-heat to 450 degrees F (I use 450 degrees F when baking baguettes).

30 minutes later

When oven has come to temperature… place pans in oven and bake for 20 minutes.

20 minutes later

Gently turn baguettes out on work surface and place on cooling rack.

Beer Bread (mini round baker – half loaves)
The purpose of this recipe is to introduce those of you who make beer bread to the no-knead method of making dough and introduce those of you who make no-knead bread to beer bread. One simple recipe with hundreds of options... change the wet ingredient—the beer—from a lager, to an amber, or a hefeweizen you can have a new and uniquely flavored bread. It's fun to experiment with beer bread... the beer isle is full of ideas.

There are two basic types of beer bread... yeast and quick. Yeast beer bread uses yeast as a leavening agent. The yeast gives the loaf an airy crumb and artisan quality. Quick beer bread uses self-rising flour which has baking soda and baking powder as leavening agents. Quick beer bread is—as the name implies— very quick and easy, but don't let that fool you. It makes delicious rolls. To see the difference between yeast and quick beer bread you may want to watch Introduction to No-Knead Beer Bread (a.k.a. Artisan Yeast Beer Bread) and Introduction to Quick Beer Bread (a.k.a. Beer Bread Dinner Rolls).

I use 2 *Lodge* cast iron mini round bakers (6") to shape these loaves... I love them. And half loaves are convenient... you can put one at each end to the table.

Beer Bread

Pour room temperature beer in a 3 to 4 qt warm glass mixing bowl (use a warm bowl… you don't want a cold bowl to take the warmth out of the beer).

>   14 oz room temperature Beer

Add salt and yeast… give a quick stir to combine.

>   1-1/2 tsp Salt
>   1-1/4 tsp Instant Yeast

Add flour… stir until dough forms a shaggy ball, scrape dry flour from side of bowl, then tumble dough to combine moist flour with dry flour.

>   3-1/2 cups Bread Flour

Place bowl in a warm draft-free location, cover with a lint-free towel (or plastic wrap), and proof for 1-1/2 hours.

1-1/2 hours later (mini round baker – half loaves)

When dough has risen and developed its gluten structure… spray mini round bakers with no-stick spray and set aside.

Start by putting handle end of spoon in center of dough and "degas, pull and stretch" dough to form a ball.

Generously dust dough and side of bowl with flour… roll dough in flour to coat.

Roll dough (and excess flour) out of bowl onto work surface.

Divide dough into 2 portions.

Then (one portion at a time) roll dough on work surface, form a ball, and place in baker.

Place bakers in a warm draft-free location, cover with a lint-free towel, and proof for 30 minutes.

Before dough is fully proofed…

Move rack to middle of oven and pre-heat to 400 degrees F.

30 minutes later

When oven has come to temperature… place bakers in oven and bake for 35 minutes.

35 minutes later

Gently turn loaves out on work surface and place on cooling rack.

Cheddar Cheese Bread (preheated Dutch oven)
Fresh from the oven bread is special... add cheese and you have a winner. Something your friends and guests will love. This is a remarkably simple recipe that everyone will enjoy.

This recipe uses the traditional no-knead method (preheated Dutch oven), baking time and temperature. And, I used a 2.6 qt *Emile Henry* flame top ceramic Dutch oven (8") to shape this loaf because it gives me a nice plump boule, but you can use any 2-1/2 qt to 5 qt Dutch oven.

Cheddar Cheese Bread

Pour warm water in a 3 to 4 qt warm glass mixing bowl (use a warm bowl… you don't want a cold bowl to take the heat out of the warm water).

    16 oz warm Water

Add salt and yeast… give a quick stir to combine.

    1-1/2 tsp Salt
    1-1/4 tsp Instant Yeast

Add flour… then cheese (if cheese is added before flour it will be harder to combine)… stir until dough forms a shaggy ball, scrape dry flour from side of bowl, then tumble dough to combine moist flour with dry flour.

    3-1/2 cups Bread Flour
    1 cup coarse shredded Cheddar Cheese

Place bowl in a warm draft-free location, cover with a lint-free towel (or plastic wrap), and proof for 1-1/2 hours.

1-1/2 hours later (preheated Dutch oven)

When dough has risen and developed its gluten structure… spray an 8" proofing skillet with no-stick cooking spray and set aside.

Start by putting handle end of spoon in center of dough and "degas, pull and stretch" dough to form a ball.

Generously dust dough and side of bowl with flour… roll dough in flour to coat.

Roll dough out of bowl into proofing skillet.

Place skillet in a warm draft-free location, cover with a lint-free towel, and proof for 30 minutes.

Before dough is fully proofed…

Move rack to lower third of the oven, place Dutch oven (with lid) in oven and pre-heat to 450 degrees F.

30 minutes later

When oven has come to temperature… remove Dutch oven from oven, transfer dough from proofing skillet to Dutch oven, shake to center, place back in oven and bake for 30 minutes with the top on.

30 minutes later

Take it out of the oven, remove top, and place back in the oven for 3 to 15 minutes to finish the crust… depending on how rustic (hard) you like your crust.

3 to 15 minutes later

Gently turn loaf out on work surface and place on cooling rack.

Multigrain Country White Bread (standard bread pan)
This is one of my most popular loaves. My first multigrain loaves used 2 cups bread flour and 1 cup wheat flour. One time I forgot the wheat flour and used 3 cups bread flour. Surprise, surprise, surprise... the multigrain country white became one of my most popular breads. I had assumed those who liked grains... liked wheat breads, but there appears to be a significant segment of our society who likes multigrain bread without the wheat bread taste. Wheat is one of those things you either like or don't like, but it doesn't mean you don't like multigrain bread.

I use a *Lodge* L4LP3 cast iron bread pan (8-1/4" x 4-1/2" x 2-1/2") to shape this loaf, but you can use any bread pan without changing baking time or temperature.

Multigrain Country White Bread

Pour warm water in a 3 to 4 qt warm glass mixing bowl (use a warm bowl... you don't want a cold bowl to take the heat out of the warm water).

    <u>16 oz warm Water</u>

Add salt, yeast and seeds... give a quick stir to combine.

    <u>1-1/2 tsp Salt</u>
    <u>1-1/4 tsp Instant Yeast</u>
    <u>1 Tbsp Sesame Seeds</u>
    <u>1 Tbsp Flax Seeds</u>

Add flour... then oats (if oats are added before flour they will absorb the water and it will be harder to combine)... stir until dough forms a shaggy ball, scrape dry flour from side of bowl, then tumble dough to combine moist flour with dry flour.

    <u>3-1/2 cups Bread Flour</u>
    <u>1/2 cup Old Fashioned Quaker Oats</u>

Place bowl in a warm draft-free location, cover with a lint-free towel (or plastic wrap), and proof for 1-1/2 hours.

1-1/2 hours later (standard bread pan - garnish)

When dough has risen and developed its gluten structure... spray an 8-1/2" x 4-1/2" bread pan with no-stick cooking spray and set aside.

Start by putting handle end of spoon in center of dough and "degas, pull and stretch" dough to form a ball.

Garnish... sprinkle dough ball and side of bowl with oats and roll to coat.

    <u>1/4 cup Old Fashioned Quaker Oats</u>

Generously dust dough and side of bowl with flour... roll dough in flour to coat. Roll dough out of bowl into bread pan.

Place pan in a warm draft-free location, cover with a lint-free towel, and proof for 30 minutes.

Before dough is fully proofed...

Move rack to middle of oven and pre-heat to 400 degrees F.

30 minutes later

When oven has come to temperature... place bread pan in oven and bake for 40 minutes.

40 minutes later

Gently turn loaf out on work surface and place on cooling rack.

Italian Sesame Sandwich Bread (poor man's Dutch oven)
For the Italian sesame sandwich bread I used "poor-man's-Dutch oven". It's the best of both worlds... the shape of sandwich bread using the principles of a Dutch oven. I used two 8-1/2" x 4-1/2" OXO bread pans, but 9" x 5" pans are perfectly acceptable.

Optional:
Add sesame and flax seed to dough... you can create an interesting appearance, texture and flavor by adding 1 Tbsp (each) sesame and flax seeds to the dough.

YouTube Video in support of recipe: No-Knead Bread 101 (Includes demonstration of Sesame Seed Bread... Italian, Muffuletta, & Sandwich) (Due to be released June 2016)

Italian Sesame Sandwich Bread

Pour warm water in a 3 to 4 qt warm glass mixing bowl (use a warm bowl… you don't want a cold bowl to take the heat out of the warm water).

    14 oz warm Water

Add salt, yeast and olive oil… give a quick stir to combine.

    1-1/2 tsp Salt
    1-1/4 tsp Instant Yeast
    1 Tbsp Extra Virgin Olive Oil
    1 Tbsp Sesame Seeds (optional)
    1 Tbsp Flax Seeds (optional)

Add flour… stir until dough forms a shaggy ball, scrape dry flour from side of bowl, then tumble dough to combine moist flour with dry flour.

    3-1/2 cups Bread Flour

Place bowl in a warm draft-free location, cover with a lint-free towel (or plastic wrap), and proof for 1-1/2 hours.

1-1/2 hours later (poor man's Dutch oven - garnish)

When dough has risen and developed its gluten structure… spray bottom pan with no-stick spray and set aside.

Start by putting handle end of spoon in center of dough and "degas, pull and stretch" dough to form a ball.

Scrape side of bowl to get remaining dough into dough ball.

Garnish… sprinkle dough with sesame seeds and roll to coat.

    2 Tbsp Sesame Seeds

Generously dust dough and side of bowl with flour, roll dough in flour to coat.

Roll dough out of bowl into bread pan.

Cover bottom bread pan with top pan and place in a warm draft-free location to proof for 30 minutes.

Before dough is fully proofed…

Move rack to lower third of oven and pre-heat to 400 degrees F.

30 minutes later

When oven has come to temperature… place "poor man's Dutch oven" in oven and bake for 40 minutes.

40 minutes later

Take pans out of the oven, remove the top, and place pan back in the oven for 3 to 15 minutes to finish the crust.

3 to 15 minutes later

Gently turn loaf out on work surface and place on cooling rack.

Italian Sesame Boule (preheated Dutch oven)

This recipe uses the traditional no-knead baking method (preheated Dutch oven), baking time and temperature. I use a 3 qt *Lodge* enameled cast iron Dutch oven (9-1/2" x 3-1/8") to shape this loaf because it gives the loaf a nice shape, but you can use any 3 to 5 qt Dutch oven.

Optional:

Add sesame and flax seed to dough... you can create an interesting appearance, texture and flavor by adding 1 Tbsp (each) sesame and flax seeds to the dough.

YouTube Video in support of recipe: No-Knead Bread 101 (Includes demonstration of Sesame Seed Bread... Italian, Muffuletta, & Sandwich) (Due to be released June 2016)

Italian Sesame Boule

Pour warm water in a 3 to 4 qt warm glass mixing bowl (use a warm bowl... you don't want a cold bowl to take the heat out of the warm water).

>14 oz warm Water

Add salt, yeast, and olive oil... give a quick stir to combine.

>1-1/2 tsp Salt
>1-1/4 tsp Instant Yeast
>1 Tbsp extra-virgin Olive Oil
>1 Tbsp Sesame Seeds (optional)
>1 Tbsp Flax Seeds (optional)

Add flour... stir until dough forms a shaggy ball, scrape dry flour from side of bowl, then tumble dough to combine moist flour with dry flour.

>3-1/2 cups Bread Flour

Place bowl in a warm draft-free location, cover with a lint-free towel (or plastic wrap), and proof for 1-1/2 hours.

1-1/2 hours later (preheated Dutch oven - garnish)

When dough has risen and developed its gluten structure... spray an 8" proofing skillet with no-stick cooking spray and set aside.

Start by putting handle end of spoon in center of dough and "degas, pull and stretch" dough to form a ball.

Garnish... sprinkle dough with sesame seeds and roll to coat.

>2 Tbsp Sesame Seeds

Generously dust dough and side of bowl with flour... roll dough in flour to coat. Roll dough out of bowl into proofing skillet.

Place skillet in a warm draft-free location, cover with a lint-free towel, and proof for 30 minutes.

Before dough is fully proofed...

Move rack to lower third of the oven, place Dutch oven in oven and pre-heat to 450 degrees F.

30 minutes later

When oven has come to temperature... remove Dutch oven from oven, transfer dough from proofing skillet to Dutch oven, shake to center, place back in oven and bake for 30 minutes with the top on.

40 minutes later

Remove top and bake for an additional 3 to 15 minutes with the top off to finish the crust.

3 to 15 minutes later

Gently turn loaf out on work surface and place on cooling rack.

Muffuletta - Sicilian Sesame Bread (9" pie pan)

"Muffuletta" (moo-foo-le-th) is both a sandwich and the low profile Sicilian sesame bread use to make the sandwich. A traditional style muffuletta sandwich consists of a muffuletta loaf split horizontally, drizzled with olive oil, covered with layers of thinly sliced meat and cheese, and dressed with olive salad.

YouTube Video in support of recipe: No-Knead Bread 101 (Includes demonstration of Sesame Seed Bread... Italian, Muffuletta, & Sandwich) (Due to be released June 2016)

Muffuletta - Sicilian Sesame Bread

Pour warm water in a 2-1/2 to 3-1/2 qt warm glass mixing bowl (use a warm bowl... you don't want a cold bowl to take the heat out of the warm water).

    8 oz warm Water

Add salt, yeast, and olive oil... give a quick stir to combine.

    1 tsp Salt
    1 tsp Instant Yeast
    2 tsp extra-virgin Olive Oil

Add flour... stir until dough forms a shaggy ball, scrape dry flour from side of bowl, then tumble dough to combine moist flour with dry flour.

    2 cups Bread Flour

Place bowl in a warm draft-free location, cover with a lint-free towel (or plastic wrap) and proof for 1-1/2 hours.

1-1/2 hours later (9" pie pan - garnish)

When dough has risen and developed its gluten structure... spray pie pan with no-stick cooking spray (or drizzle with olive oil) and set aside.

Start by putting handle end of spoon in center of dough and "degas, pull and stretch" dough to form a ball.

Garnish... sprinkle dough and side of bowl with seeds and roll to coat.

    2 Tbsp Sesame Seeds

Generously dust dough and side of bowl with flour... roll dough in flour to coat.

    1 Tbsp Flour

Roll dough out of bowl into pie plate and shape into a 9" flat disc. If the dough is springy and difficult to shape... cover with a lint-free towel, rest for 10 minutes (resting dough makes it easier to shape dough), and finish shaping.

Place pan in a warm draft-free location, cover with a lint-free towel, and proof for 30 minutes.

Before dough is fully proofed...

Move rack to middle of oven and pre-heat to 400 degrees F.

30 minutes later

When oven has come to temperature... place pan in oven and bake for 30 minutes.

30 minutes later

Gently turn loaf out on work surface and place on cooling rack.

Honey Oatmeal Bread (uncovered baker)

Fresh from the oven bread with the wholesome goodness of oats and the sweetness of honey... what's not to like? This loaf is as delicious to eat as it is pleasing to the eye and the garnish is very easy to apply giving the loaf a special appearance.

I used a 2 qt *Threshold* stoneware oval baker (10" x 6-3/4" x 2-1/2") to shape the loaf, but any oven-proof dish will work. I like casserole dishes with rounded bottoms… they give loaves a nice shape.

Honey Oatmeal Bread

Pour warm water in a 3 to 4 qt warm glass mixing bowl (use a warm bowl... you don't want a cold bowl to take the heat out of the warm water).

 16 oz warm Water

Add salt, yeast, olive oil and honey... give a quick stir to combine.

 1-1/2 tsp Salt
 1-1/4 tsp Instant Yeast
 1 Tbsp extra-virgin Olive Oil
 1 Tbsp Honey

Add flour... then oats (if oats are added before flour they will absorb the water and it will be harder to combine)... stir until dough forms a shaggy ball, scrape dry flour from side of bowl, then tumble dough to combine moist flour with dry flour.

 3-1/2 cups Bread Flour
 1 cup Old Fashioned Quaker Oats

Place bowl in a warm draft-free location, cover with a lint-free towel (or plastic wrap), and proof for 1-1/2 hours.

1-1/2 hours later (uncovered baker - garnish)

When dough has risen and developed its gluten structure... spray baker with no-stick cooking spray and set aside.

Start by putting handle end of spoon in center of dough and "degas, pull and stretch" dough to form a ball.

Garnish... sprinkle dough and side of bowl with oats and roll to coat.

 1/4 cup Old Fashioned Quaker Oats

Generously dust dough and side of bowl with flour... roll dough in flour to coat. Roll dough out of bowl into baker.

Place baker in a warm draft-free location, cover with a lint-free towel, and proof for 30 minutes.

Before dough is fully proofed...

Move rack to middle of oven and pre-heat to 400 degrees F.

30 minutes later

When oven has come to temperature... place baker in oven and bake for 40 minutes.

40 minutes later

Gently turn loaf out on work surface and place on cooling rack.

Honey Whole Wheat Bread (preheated Dutch oven)
This whole wheat recipe balances the nutrition and nutty taste of whole wheat with the crumb of a Country White in a hearty, moist loaf with a touch of honey for sweetness.

Because whole wheat flour has less gluten... 100% whole wheat loaves can be a little too heavy and dense for some tastes. Personally, I like to balance the nutritional value of whole wheat with the crumb and texture of bread flour by using a 50/50 blend. And I used a total of 4 cups flour to create the size loaf I desired.

This recipe uses the traditional no-knead method (preheated Dutch oven), baking time and temperature. And, I use a 3 qt *Lodge* enameled cast iron Dutch oven (9-1/2" x 3-1/8") to shape this loaf because it gives the loaf a nice shape, but you can use any 2-1/2 qt to 5 qt Dutch oven.

Honey Whole Wheat Bread

Pour warm water in a 3 to 4 qt warm glass mixing bowl (use a warm bowl… you don't want a cold bowl to take the heat out of the warm water).

<u>16 oz warm Water</u>

Add salt, yeast, olive oil and honey… give a quick stir to combine.

<u>1-1/2 tsp Salt</u>
<u>1-1/4 tsp Instant Yeast</u>
<u>1 Tbsp extra-virgin Olive Oil</u>
<u>1 Tbsp Honey</u>

Add flour… stir until dough forms a shaggy ball, scrape dry flour from side of bowl, then tumble dough to combine moist flour with dry flour.

<u>2 cups Bread Flour</u>
<u>2 cups Whole Wheat Flour</u>

Place bowl in a warm draft-free location, cover with a lint-free towel (or plastic wrap), and proof for 1-1/2 hours.

1-1/2 hours later (preheated Dutch oven)

When dough has risen and developed its gluten structure… spray an 8" proofing skillet with no-stick cooking spray and set aside.

Start by putting handle end of spoon in center of dough and "degas, pull and stretch" dough to form a ball.

Generously dust dough and side of bowl with flour… roll dough in flour to coat.

Roll dough out of bowl into proofing skillet.

Place skillet in a warm draft-free location, cover with a lint-free towel, and proof for 30 minutes.

Before dough is fully proofed…

Move rack to lower third of the oven, place Dutch oven (with lid) in oven and pre-heat to 450 degrees F.

30 minutes later

When oven has come to temperature… remove Dutch oven from oven, transfer dough from proofing skillet to Dutch oven, shake to center, place back in oven and bake for 30 minutes with the top on.

30 minutes later

Take it out of the oven, remove top, and place back in the oven for 3 to 15 minutes to finish the crust… depending on how rustic (hard) you like your crust.

3 to 15 minutes later

Gently turn loaf out on work surface and place on cooling rack.

Harvest 8 Grain Whole Wheat Bread (long covered baker)
This Harvest 8 Grain Wheat Bread has a more robust and complex flavor than the multigrain country white and wheat breads. I experimented with and tested a number of my own multigrain mixtures before I discovered King Arthur's Harvest Grains Blend and (as they state on their website) the whole oat berries, millet, rye flakes and wheat flakes enhance texture while the flax, poppy, sesame, and sunflower seeds add crunch and great, nutty flavor. Wow, the flavor is great... and it's a lot easier and... more practical... to purchase a blend of seeds. You should experiment with blends available in your community.

I use a *Sassafras* superstone oblong covered baker (13-1/2" x 4-1/2" x 2-1/2") to shape this loaf. No special reason... just a good change of pace.

Harvest 8 Grain Whole Wheat Bread

Pour warm water in a 3 to 4 qt warm glass mixing bowl (use a warm bowl… you don't want a cold bowl to take the heat out of the warm water).

    16 oz warm Water

Add salt, yeast, grains and olive oil… give a quick stir to combine.

    1-1/2 tsp Salt
    1-1/4 tsp Instant Yeast
    2/3 cup King Arthur Harvest Grains Blend
    1 Tbsp extra-virgin Olive Oil

Add flour… stir until dough forms a shaggy ball, scrape dry flour from side of bowl, then tumble dough to combine moist flour with dry flour.

    2 cups Bread Flour
    2 cups Whole Wheat Flour

Place bowl in a warm draft-free location, cover with a lint-free towel (or plastic wrap), and proof for 1-1/2 hours.

1-1/2 hours later (long covered baker)

When dough has risen and developed its gluten structure… spray baker with no-stick spray and set aside (if baker is new use "preheated Dutch oven" method until bakers is seasoned or the loaf may have a tendency to stick).

Start by putting handle end of spoon in center of dough and "degas, pull and stretch" dough to form a ball.

Generously dust dough and side of bowl with flour… roll dough in flour to coat.

Roll dough (and excess flour) out of bowl onto work surface, roll dough on work surface in flour to shape, and place in baker.

Place baker in a warm draft-free location, cover with lid, and proof for 30 minutes.

Before dough is fully proofed…

Move rack to lower third of the oven and pre-heat to 400 degrees F (this method does not require you to preheat baker).

30 minutes later

When oven has come to temperature… place baker in oven and bake for 40 minutes with the top on.

40 minutes later

Take it out of the oven, remove top, and place back in the oven for 3 to 15 minutes to finish the crust… depending on how rustic (hard) you like your crust.

3 to 15 minutes later

Gently turn loaf out on work surface and place on cooling rack.

Flax Seed 8 Grain Bread (standard bread pan)
This loaf combines the nutrition of milled flax seed (high in fiber and omega-3 fatty acids plus lignans) with whole oat berries, millet, rye flakes, wheat flakes, poppy seeds, sesame seeds, and sunflower seeds (King Arthur's Harvest Blend). The flavor is great.

I used a *Chicago Metallic* bread pan (8-1/2" x 4-1/2") to shape this loaf... the bread pan is the #1 baking vessel for bread (most common), but you can use any anything from a preheated Dutch oven (the traditional no-knead method) to an uncovered baker.

Flax Seed 8 Grain Bread

Pour warm water in a 3 to 4 qt warm glass mixing bowl (use a warm bowl... you don't want a cold bowl to take the heat out of the warm water).

>16 oz warm Water

Add salt, yeast, grains, olive oil and honey... give a quick stir to combine.

>1-1/2 tsp Salt
>1-1/4 tsp Instant Yeast
>2/3 cup King Arthur Harvest Grains Blend
>1 Tbsp Flax Seeds
>1 Tbsp extra-virgin Olive Oil
>1 Tbsp Honey

Add flour... stir until dough forms a shaggy ball, scrape dry flour from side of bowl, then tumble dough to combine moist flour with dry flour.

>2 cups Bread Flour
>1-1/2 cups Whole Wheat Flour
>1/2 cup Milled Flax Seed

Place bowl in a warm draft-free location, cover with a lint-free towel (or plastic wrap), and proof for 1-1/2 hours.

1-1/2 hours later (standard bread pan - baste)

When dough has risen and developed its gluten structure... spray an 8-1/2" x 4-1/2" bread pan with no-stick cooking spray and set aside.

Start by putting handle end of spoon in center of dough and "degas, pull and stretch" dough to form a ball.

Baste... drizzle dough and side of bowl with olive oil... roll dough in oil to coat.

>1 Tbsp Olive Oil

Roll dough out of bowl into bread pan.

Place pan in a warm draft-free location, cover with a lint-free towel, and proof for 30 minutes.

Before dough is fully proofed...

Move rack to middle of oven and pre-heat to 400 degrees F.

30 minutes later

When oven has come to temperature... place bread pan in oven and bake for 40 minutes.

40 minutes later

Gently turn loaf out on work surface and place on cooling rack.

Rosemary Bread (mini round baker – half loaves)

I was so thrilled with the appetizer loaves at *Macaroni Grill* that I decided to make my own and developed a rosemary demi loaf recipe that required kneading. Then my wife found a no-knead ciabatta bread recipe in the local newspaper… I was converted. I experimented with no-knead recipes and converted my old rosemary demi loaf recipe to the no-knead method. That was the beginning and I haven't looked back.

I use 2 *Lodge* cast iron mini round bakers (6") to shape these loaves… the cast iron bakers make the loaves look special.

Rosemary Bread

Pour warm water in a 3 to 4 qt warm glass mixing bowl (use a warm bowl... you don't want a cold bowl to take the heat out of the warm water).

    14 oz warm Water

Add salt, yeast, rosemary and olive oil... give a quick stir to combine.

    1-1/2 tsp Salt
    1-1/4 tsp Instant Yeast
    1 Tbsp dried Rosemary
    1 Tbsp extra-virgin Olive Oil

Add flour... stir until dough forms a shaggy ball, scrape dry flour from side of bowl, then tumble dough to combine moist flour with dry flour.

    3-1/2 cups Bread Flour

Place bowl in a warm draft-free location, cover with a lint-free towel (or plastic wrap), and proof for 1-1/2 hours.

1-1/2 hours later (mini round baker – half loaves)

When dough has risen and developed its gluten structure... spray mini round bakers with no-stick spray and set aside.

Start by putting handle end of spoon in center of dough and "degas, pull and stretch" dough to form a ball.

Generously dust dough and side of bowl with flour... roll dough in flour to coat.

Roll dough (and excess flour) out of bowl onto work surface.

Divide dough into 2 portions.

Then (one portion at a time) roll dough on work surface, form a ball, and place in baker.

Place bakers in a warm draft-free location, cover with a lint-free towel, and proof for 30 minutes.

Before dough is fully proofed...

Move rack to middle of oven and pre-heat to 400 degrees F.

30 minutes later

When oven has come to temperature... place bakers in oven and bake for 35 minutes.

35 minutes later

Gently turn loaves out on work surface and place on cooling rack.

Caraway Rye Bread (standard bread pan)

This is a rustic rye bread, with a mild rye flavor and a generous amount of caraway seeds that would be the perfect complement to a pastrami sandwich.

I use a *USA Pan* heavy gage aluminized steel bread pan (8-1/2" x 4-1/2") to shape this loaf because I like to use rye bread for sandwiches, but you can use any anything from a preheated Dutch oven (the traditional no-knead method) to an uncovered baker.

Caraway Rye Bread

Pour warm water in a 3 to 4 qt warm glass mixing bowl (use a warm bowl... you don't want a cold bowl to take the heat out of the warm water).

    14 oz warm Water

Add salt, yeast, sugar, seeds and olive oil... give a quick stir to combine.

    1-1/2 tsp Salt
    1-1/4 tsp Instant Yeast
    1 Tbsp Sugar
    2 Tbsp Caraway Seeds
    1 Tbsp extra-virgin Olive Oil

Add flour... stir until dough forms a shaggy ball, scrape dry flour from side of bowl, then tumble dough to combine moist flour with dry flour.

    2-1/2 cups Bread Flour
    1 cup Rye Flour

Place bowl in a warm draft-free location, cover with a lint-free towel (or plastic wrap), and proof for 1-1/2 hours.

1-1/2 hours later (standard bread pan)

When dough has risen and developed its gluten structure... spray an 8-1/2" x 4-1/2" bread pan with no-stick cooking spray and set aside.

Start by putting handle end of spoon in center of dough and "degas, pull and stretch" dough to form a ball.

Generously dust dough and side of bowl with flour... roll dough in flour to coat. Roll dough out of bowl into bread pan.

Place pan in a warm draft-free location, cover with a lint-free towel, and proof for 30 minutes.

Before dough is fully proofed...

Move rack to middle of oven and pre-heat to 400 degrees F.

30 minutes later

When oven has come to temperature... place bread pan in oven and bake for 40 minutes.

40 minutes later

Gently turn loaf out on work surface and place on cooling rack.

Polenta Bread (preheated uncovered baker)

The term "polenta" is of Italian origin, but polenta (corn grits) is a Native American grain that was not cultivated in Europe until the early 1500's (after Columbus). Coarse ground grits (polenta) adds texture and a depth of flavor which makes very special bread.

I used an *Emerson Creek Pottery* bread baking bowl (2-3/4" x 8") to shape this loaf. According to King Arthur Flour, "For best results, treat your stoneware pan with care. Oil your stoneware pan with neutral-flavored vegetable oil before each use; a nice patina will develop over time. For additional prevention of sticking, sprinkle a thin layer of cornmeal or semolina into the bottom of the oiled pan." And I agree with their suggestions, but I still had a problem with dough sticking. I found it best to preheat the bowl and spray it with no-stick spray until it was seasoned. That is why I am using the bread baking bowl as the example for "preheated uncovered baker".

Polenta Bread

Pour warm water in a 3 to 4 qt warm glass mixing bowl (use a warm bowl... you don't want a cold bowl to take the heat out of the warm water).

    14 oz warm Water

Add salt, yeast, seeds and olive oil... give a quick stir to combine.

    1-1/2 tsp Salt
    1-1/4 tsp Instant Yeast
    1 Tbsp Sesame Seeds
    1 Tbsp Flax Seeds
    1 Tbsp Olive Oil

Add flour... then polenta... stir until dough forms a shaggy ball, scrape dry flour from side of bowl, then tumble dough to combine moist flour with dry flour.

    3-1/2 cups Bread Flour
    1/3 cup Bob's Red Mill Corn Grits (a.k.a. Polenta)

Place bowl in a warm draft-free location, cover with a lint-free towel (or plastic wrap), and proof for 1-1/2 hours.

1-1/2 hours later (preheated uncovered baker – garnish & baste)

When dough has risen and developed its gluten structure... spray an 8" proofing skillet with no-stick cooking spray and set aside.

Start by putting handle end of spoon in center of dough and "degas, pull and stretch" dough to form a ball.

Garnish (optional)... sprinkle dough ball and side of bowl with polenta... roll to coat.

    2 Tbsp Bob's Red Mill Corn Grits (a.k.a. Polenta)

Baste... drizzle dough and side of bowl with olive oil... roll dough in oil to coat.

    1 Tbsp Olive Oil

Roll dough out of bowl into proofing skillet.

Place skillet in a warm draft-free location, cover with a lint-free towel, and proof for 30 minutes.

Before dough is fully proofed...

Move rack to middle of oven, place baker in oven and pre-heat to 400 degrees F.

30 minutes later

When oven has come to temperature... remove baker from oven, transfer dough from proofing skillet to baker, shake to center, place baker back in oven and bake for 40 to 50 minutes (polenta bread typically has a more rustic crust).

40 to 50 minutes later

Gently turn loaf out on work surface and place on cooling rack.

Mediterranean Olive Bread (long loaf pan – half loaves)

If you like Mediterranean flavors you'll love this bread. It's unique... it's different... it's perfect for that special occasion. If a restaurant served you this loaf as their signature bread... you'd be talking about it for years and it's surprisingly easy it is to make.

I like Mediterranean olive loaves to be long and narrow so I divided the dough in half and used 2 *Wilton* long loaf pans (12" x 4-1/2" x 3-1/8") to shape them. Then we sliced it and served it as an appetizer with cream cheese, pimento cheese spread, deli meat, provolone, etc.

Mediterranean Olive Bread

Prepare flavor ingredients... zest lemon, slice green olives in half, slice kalamata olives in thirds, and set aside.

    Zest of 1 Lemon
    2-1/4 oz (1 can) sliced Black Olives
    1 can stuffed Green Olives (use black olive can to measure)
    1 can Pitted Kalamata Olives (use black olive can to measure)

Pour warm water in a 3 to 4 qt warm glass mixing bowl (use a warm bowl... you don't want a cold bowl to take the heat out of the warm water).

    12 oz warm Water

Add salt, yeast, thyme, and olive oil... give a quick stir to combine.

    1-1/2 tsp Salt
    1-1/4 tsp Instant Yeast
    1 tsp dried Thyme
    1 Tbsp extra-virgin Olive Oil

Add flour... then flavor ingredients. Stir until dough forms a shaggy ball, scrape dry flour from side of bowl, then tumble dough to combine moist flour with dry flour.

    3-1/2 cups Bread Flour

Place bowl in a warm draft-free location, cover with a lint-free towel (or plastic wrap), and proof for 1-1/2 hours.

1-1/2 hours later (long loaf pan – half loaves)

When dough has risen and developed its gluten structure... spray 2 long bread pans (12" x 4-1/2" x 3-1/8") with no-stick cooking spray and set aside.

Start by putting handle end of spoon in center of dough and "degas, pull and stretch" dough to form a ball.

Generously dust dough and side of bowl with flour... roll dough in flour to coat.

Roll dough (and excess flour) out of bowl onto work surface.

Divide dough into 2 portions.

Then (one portion at a time) roll dough on work surface in flour to shape... place in pan.

Place pans in a warm draft-free location, cover with a lint-free towel, and proof for 30 minutes.

Before dough is fully proofed...

Move rack to middle of oven and pre-heat to 400 degrees F.

30 minutes later

When oven has come to temperature... place pans in oven and bake for 35 minutes.

35 minutes later

Gently turn loaf out on work surface and place on cooling rack.

Mexican Jalapeño-Chili Fiesta Bread (preheated uncovered baker)
Celebrate the flavors of a fiesta with this Jalapeño-Chili bread. If you like jalapeño and chilies… you'll love this loaf.

I used an *Emerson Creek Pottery* bread baking bowl (2-3/4" x 8") to shape this loaf. According to King Arthur Flour, "For best results, treat your stoneware pan with care. Oil your stoneware pan with neutral-flavored vegetable oil before each use; a nice patina will develop over time. For additional prevention of sticking, sprinkle a thin layer of cornmeal or semolina into the bottom of the oiled pan." And I agree with their suggestions, but I still had a problem with dough sticking. I found it best to preheat the bowl and spray it with no-stick spray until it was seasoned. That is why I am using the bread baking bowl as the example for "preheated covered baker".

Mexican Jalapeño-Chili Fiesta Bread

Pour warm water in a 3 to 4 qt warm glass mixing bowl (use a warm bowl… you don't want a cold bowl to take the heat out of the warm water).

    12 oz warm Water

Add salt, yeast, chilies, peppers, corn, and olive oil… give a quick stir to combine.

    1-1/2 tsp Salt
    1-1/4 tsp Instant Yeast
    2 whole Green Chilies (diced)
    1/2 cup sliced Jalapeño Peppers
    1/2 cup Golden Sweet Corn
    1 Tbsp extra-virgin Olive Oil

Add flour… then cheese… stir until dough forms a shaggy ball, scrape dry flour from side of bowl, then tumble dough to combine moist flour with dry flour.

    3-1/2 cups Bread Flour
    3 slices Pepper Jack Cheese (diced)

Place bowl in a warm draft-free location, cover with a lint-free towel (or plastic wrap), and proof for 1-1/2 hours.

1-1/2 hours later (preheated uncovered baker - baste)

When dough has risen and developed its gluten structure… spray an 8" proofing skillet with no-stick cooking spray and set aside.

Start by putting handle end of spoon in center of dough and "degas, pull and stretch" dough to form a ball.

Baste… drizzle dough and side of bowl with oil and roll to coat.

    1 Tbsp Vegetable Oil

Roll dough out of bowl into proofing skillet.

Place skillet in a warm draft-free location, cover with a lint-free towel, and proof for 30 minutes.

Before dough is fully proofed…

Move rack to middle of oven, place baker in oven and pre-heat to 400 degrees F.

30 minutes later

When oven has come to temperature… remove baker from oven, transfer dough from proofing skillet to baker, shake to center, place baker back in oven and bake for 50 minutes (bake time was increased 10 minutes because peppers, chilies, corn, etc. added moisture which needs to bake out).

50 minutes later

Gently turn loaf out on work surface and place on cooling rack.

Buttermilk Bread (long covered baker)

If you like buttermilk ranch dressing... you'll like buttermilk bread. And this isn't the average buttermilk bread... this is an artisan loaf with an airy crumb and tender crust. The appearance is excellent... the taste is great. Buttermilk is a great all-purpose bread. Buttermilk gives it a rich tangy flavor with a subtle buttery depth that is great for sandwiches and toast.

It is a common misconception to associate buttermilk with the richness of butter but... buttermilk does not have butterfat. Buttermilk is the liquid remaining after taking the butter fat out of the milk in the process of making butter, thus it is lower in calories and fat than butter and higher in calcium, vitamin B12 and potassium than regular milk. And it's important to use cultured buttermilk, if you substitute 2% for cultured buttermilk in this recipe it will upset the balance of wet and dry ingredients (it's thinner), and you don't want to lose the nutritional value of buttermilk. After all, you wouldn't want to take the "yo" out of yogurt.

I used a *Sassafras* superstone oblong covered baker (13-1/2" x 4-1/2" x 2-1/2") to shape and bake this loaf because the crust of buttermilk bread has a tendency to turn dark brown and the cover will protect the crust... then I can control the color when I remove the cover to finish baking.

Buttermilk Bread

Pour buttermilk and water to a 3 to 4 qt glass mixing bowl and microwave on high for 1 minute.

 8 oz Cultured Buttermilk
 6 oz warm Water

Add salt, yeast, sugar and oil… give a quick stir to combine.

 1-1/2 tsp Salt
 1-1/4 tsp Instant Yeast
 1 Tbsp Sugar
 1 Tbsp Vegetable Oil

Add flour… stir until dough forms a shaggy ball, scrape dry flour from side of bowl, then tumble dough to combine moist flour with dry flour.

 3-1/2 cups Bread Flour

Place bowl in a warm draft-free location, cover with a lint-free towel (or plastic wrap), and proof for 1-1/2 hours.

1-1/2 hours later (long covered baker – garnish)

When dough has risen and developed its gluten structure… spray baker with no-stick spray and set aside (if baker is new use "preheated Dutch oven" method until bakers is seasoned or the loaf may have a tendency to stick).

Start by putting handle end of spoon in center of dough and "degas, pull and stretch" dough to form a ball.

Garnish… sprinkle dough and side of bowl with seeds and roll to coat.

 2 Tbsp Sesame Seeds

Generously dust dough and side of bowl with flour… roll dough in flour to coat.

Roll dough out of bowl into baker and cover with lid.

Place baker in a warm draft-free location and proof for 30 minutes.

Before dough is fully proofed…

Move rack to lower third of the oven and pre-heat to 400 degrees F (this method does not require you to preheat baker).

30 minutes later

When oven has come to temperature… place baker in oven and bake for 40 minutes with the top on.

40 minutes later

Take it out of the oven, remove top, and place back in the oven for 3 to 15 minutes to finish the crust… depending on how rustic (hard) you like your crust.

3 to 15 minutes later

Gently turn loaf out on work surface and place on cooling rack.

Cinnamon Raisin Bread (small bread pan)
Homemade fresh from the oven cinnamon raisin bread is a great way to start your day and when our guests stay overnight, my wife wants them to wake up to the aroma of fresh for the oven cinnamon raisin bread filling the house.

I used a *Good Cook* premium nonstick bread pan (8" x 4" x 2-1/4") to shape this loaf. Raisin bread is ideally suited for a smaller bread pan.

Cinnamon Raisin Bread

Pour warm water in a 3 to 4 qt warm glass mixing bowl (use a warm bowl… you don't want a cold bowl to take the heat out of the warm water).

> 14 oz warm Water

Add salt, yeast, sugar, and cinnamon… give a quick stir to combine with a flat whisk or fork (it will make it easier to combine the cinnamon).

> 1-1/2 tsp Salt
> 1-1/4 tsp Instant Yeast
> 2 Tbsp Brown Sugar
> 1 Tbsp ground Cinnamon

Add flour… then raisins. Stir until dough forms a shaggy ball, scrape dry flour from side of bowl, then tumble dough to combine moist flour with dry flour.

> 3 cups Bread Flour
> 1 cup Raisins

Place bowl in a warm draft-free location, cover with a lint-free towel (or plastic wrap), and proof for 1-1/2 hours.

1-1/2 hours later (small bread pan)

When dough has risen and developed its gluten structure… spray an 8" x 4" bread pan with no-stick cooking spray and set aside.

Start by putting handle end of spoon in center of dough and "degas, pull and stretch" dough to form a ball.

Generously dust dough and side of bowl with flour (optional)… roll dough in flour to coat.

Scrape dough out of bowl into bread pan.

Place pan in a warm draft-free location, cover with a lint-free towel, and proof for 30 minutes.

Before dough is fully proofed…

Move rack to middle of oven and pre-heat to 400 degrees F.

30 minutes later

When oven has come to temperature… place loaf pan in the oven and bake for 50 minutes (typically I would bake a standard 3 cup loaf in a 4" x 8" bread pan for 40 minutes, but raisin bread may need to be baked for an additional 5 to 10 minutes because of the moisture and density of the raisins).

50 minutes later

Gently turn loaf out on to the work surface and place on a cooling rack (cooling racks allow the bottom of the loaf to air dry).

English Muffin Loaf (small bread pan)

This English muffin loaf is unique... a specialty loaf with its own method. It has two leavening agents... yeast and baking soda... and is prepared more in the style of a quick bread. Makes excellent toast for breakfast.

I used a *Good Cook* premium nonstick bread pan (8" x 4" x 2-1/4") to shape this loaf... the slices will fit nicely in a toaster.

English Muffin Loaf (small bread pan – specialty bread)
Spray small bread pan (8" x 4") with no-stick cooking spray and set aside.
Pour water and milk to a 3 to 4 qt glass mixing bowl and microwave on high for 1 minute.
      4 oz warm Water
      8 oz Whole Milk
Add salt, yeast, sugar, baking soda and oil… give a quick stir to combine.
      1-1/2 tsp Salt
      1 Tbsp Instant Yeast
      1-1/2 tsp Sugar
      1/2 tsp Baking Soda
      1 Tbsp Vegetable Oil
Add flour… stir until dough forms a shaggy ball, scrape dry flour from side of bowl, then tumble dough to combine moist flour with dry flour.
      3 cups Bread Flour
Use a spatula to shape dough into a ball.
Garnish… sprinkle dough ball and side of bowl with cornmeal and roll to coat.
      1 Tbsp Yellow Cornmeal
Generously dust dough and side of bowl with flour… roll dough in flour to coat.
Roll dough out of bowl into bread pan.
Place pan in a warm draft-free location, cover with a lint-free towel, and proof for 1 hour.

45 minutes later
Before muffin dough has fully proofed… move rack to middle of oven and pre-heat to 400 degrees F.

15 minutes later
When oven has come to temperature… place pan in oven and bake for 30 minutes.

30 minutes later
Gently turn loaf out on work surface and place on cooling rack.

We are attracted to no-knead bread because
it's easy and convenient.
And many of us don't make rolls because
we don't want the hassle of shaping rolls.

Good news...
you can use the bakeware to shape the rolls for you.
Just plop the dough into the bakeware
and let Mother Nature do her magic for you.

Rolls & Buns

Bread is an important part of the meal... it starts the dining experience. Good rolls... good restaurant. Great rolls... great restaurant. Likewise, fresh from the oven rolls can elevate your dining experience.

To further expand your repertoire, these recipes have a dual purpose… ingredients for specific breads and technique for shaping rolls using a style or bakeware. The recipes use…

Jumbo muffin pan
Pull-apart
Muffin cutter
Hand shaped
Mini round cake pans
Baguette pans
Mini loaf pans

And, you can use the ingredients from one recipe and the technique from another. The options are endless.

Traditional Dinner Rolls (jumbo muffin pans)
These dinner rolls are simple and basic. If you're making your first batch of rolls this is the place to start... the rolls don't require any shaping. Just "plop" the dough in a jumbo muffin pan and the pan will shape the rolls for you. I used 2 *Wilton* jumbo muffin pans to shape the rolls.

YouTube video in support of recipe: Introduction to No-Knead Turbo Rolls (World's Easiest Dinner Rolls... Ready to Bake in 2-1/2 Hours)

Traditional Dinner Rolls

Pour warm water in a 3 to 4 qt warm glass mixing bowl (use a warm bowl... you don't want a cold bowl to take the heat out of the warm water).

<u>14 oz warm Water</u>

Add salt and yeast... give a quick stir to combine.

<u>1-1/2 tsp Salt</u>
<u>1-1/4 tsp Instant Yeast</u>

Add flour... stir until dough forms a shaggy ball, scrape dry flour from side of bowl, then tumble dough to combine moist flour with dry flour.

<u>3-1/2 cups Bread Flour</u>

Place bowl in a warm draft-free location, cover with a lint-free towel (or plastic wrap), and proof for 1-1/2 hours.

1-1/2 hours later (jumbo muffin pan)

When dough has risen and developed its gluten structure... spray 8 cavities in 2 jumbo muffin pans with no-stick cooking spray and set aside.

Start by putting handle end of spoon in center of dough and "degas, pull and stretch" dough to form a ball.

Generously dust dough and side of bowl with flour... roll dough in flour to coat.

Roll dough (and excess flour) out of bowl onto work surface.

Press lightly to flatten... then divide dough into 8 portions (as you would a pizza) and place 1 portion in each cavity (cavity will shape roll for you).

Place pans in a warm draft-free location, cover with a lint-free towel, and proof for 30 minutes.

Before dough is fully proofed...

Move rack to middle of oven and pre-heat to 450 degrees F.

30 minutes later

When oven has come to temperature... place pans in oven and bake for 20 minutes.

20 minutes later

Gently turn rolls out on work surface and place on cooling rack.

Pull-Apart Dinner Rolls (pull-apart - baste)
One of the beauties of this recipe is that you don't have to handle, shape or move the rolls from the work surface. Use a rolling pin to spread the dough, divide into sections with a pizza cutter and "poof"... you have pull-apart dinner rolls. I used a standard non-stick silicone baking mat (11" x 16-1/2") for the work surface and baking, but you can also use a cookie sheet.

Pull-Apart Dinner Rolls

Pour warm water in a 3 to 4 qt warm glass mixing bowl (use a warm bowl... you don't want a cold bowl to take the heat out of the warm water).

> 14 oz warm Water

Add salt and yeast... give a quick stir to combine.

> 1-1/2 tsp Salt
> 1-1/4 tsp Instant Yeast

Add flour... stir until dough forms a shaggy ball, scrape dry flour from side of bowl, then tumble dough to combine moist flour with dry flour.

> 3-1/2 cups Bread Flour

Place bowl in a warm draft-free location, cover with a lint-free towel (or plastic wrap), and proof for 1-1/2 hours.

1-1/2 hours later (pull-apart - baste)

When dough has risen and developed its gluten structure... place silicone baking mat on work surface.

Start by putting handle end of spoon in center of dough and "degas, pull and stretch" dough to form a ball.

Baste... drizzle dough and side of bowl with oil... roll dough in oil to coat.

> 1 Tbsp Vegetable Oil

Roll dough (and excess oil) out of bowl onto silicone baking mat.

Use a rolling pin to spread dough until it covers 80% of the mat.

Then use a pizza cutter (be careful not to cut through the mat) to divide the dough into sections.

Slide cookie sheet under silicone baking mat, place in a warm draft-free location, cover with a lint-free towel, and proof for 30 minutes.

Before dough is fully proofed...

Move rack to middle of oven and pre-heat to 450 degrees F.

30 minutes later

When oven has come to temperature... place cookie sheet in oven and bake for 20 minutes.

20 minutes later

Gently turn rolls out on work surface and place on cooling rack.

Garlic-Cheese Rolls (muffin cutter)

Bread is one of the great comfort foods and fresh from the oven bread is special, add cheese and garlic... you'll have a winner. Something your friends and guests will love.

This recipe uses a biscuit cutter to shape the rolls... it's simple. Just roll the dough to a uniform thickness, cut the rolls out with a biscuit cutter (just as you would when making biscuits), and bake on parchment paper, silicone baking mat or cookie sheet. Then I took the excess dough and made bread sticks. It might look a little like a chicken leg, but it's a bread stick and they're usually the first to go.

Garlic-Cheese Rolls

Pour warm water in a 3 to 4 qt warm glass mixing bowl (use a warm bowl... you don't want a cold bowl to take the heat out of the warm water).

    14 oz warm Water

Add salt, yeast, and garlic... give a quick stir to combine.

    1-1/2 tsp Salt
    1-1/4 tsp Instant Yeast
    1 to 2 tsp Garlic Paste or minced Garlic

Add flour... then cheese... (if cheese is added before flour it can clump and it will be harder to distribute evenly) and stir until dough forms a shaggy ball, scrape dry flour from side of bowl, then tumble dough to combine moist flour with dry flour.

    3-1/2 cups Bread Flour
    1 cup coarsely shredded Cheddar Cheese

Place bowl in a warm draft-free location, cover with a lint-free towel (or plastic wrap), and proof for 1-1/2 hours.

1-1/2 hours later (muffin cutter)

When dough has risen and developed its gluten structure... place silicone baking mat on cookie sheet and set aside. (It is not necessary to spray the silicone baking mat with no stick spray, but you would need to if you baked directly on the cookie sheet.)

Start by putting handle end of spoon in center of dough and "degas, pull and stretch" dough to form a ball.

Generously dust dough and side of bowl with flour... roll dough in flour to coat.

Roll dough (and excess flour) out of bowl onto work surface.

Firmly press to spread and form a 12" circle... then take a 2-1/2" to 3" round cutter, cut rolls, and place rolls on the silicone baking mat (just as you would muffins).

Place in a warm draft-free location, cover with a lint-free towel, and proof for 30 minutes.

Before dough is fully proofed...

Move rack to middle of oven and pre-heat to 450 degrees F.

30 minutes later

When oven has come to temperature... place pans in oven and bake for 20 minutes.

20 minutes later

Gently turn rolls out on work surface and place on cooling rack.

Multigrain Country White Rolls (hand shaped)
My first multigrain loaves used 2 cups bread flour and 1 cup wheat flour. One day I forgot the wheat flour and used 3 cups bread flour. Surprise, surprise, surprise... the multigrain country white became one of my most requested breads. I had assumed those who like multigrain also like whole wheat, but there appears to be a significant segment of our society who likes multigrain bread without the whole wheat taste. Wheat is one of those things you either like or don't like, but it doesn't mean you don't like multigrain bread.

Most of the recipes in this cookbook use bakeware to shape the rolls and buns, but they can be shaped by hand. This recipe is an example. These rolls can be baked on parchment paper, silicone baking mat or cookie sheet.

Multigrain Country White Rolls

Pour warm water in a 3 to 4 qt warm glass mixing bowl (use a warm bowl... you don't want a cold bowl to take the heat out of the warm water).

> 16 oz warm Water

Add salt, yeast, seeds and olive oil... give a quick stir to combine.

> 1-1/2 tsp Salt
> 1-1/4 tsp Instant Yeast
> 1 Tbsp Sesame Seeds
> 1 Tbsp Flax Seeds
> 1 Tbsp extra-virgin Olive Oil

Add flour... then oats... (if oats are added before flour they will absorb the water and it will be harder to combine) and stir until dough forms a shaggy ball, scrape dry flour from side of bowl, then tumble dough to combine moist flour with dry flour.

> 3-1/2 cups Bread Flour
> 1/2 cup Old Fashioned Quaker Oats

Place bowl in a warm draft-free location, cover with a lint-free towel (or plastic wrap), and proof for 1-1/2 hours.

1-1/2 hours later (hand shaped)

When dough has risen and developed its gluten structure... place silicone baking mat on cookie sheet and set aside. (It is not necessary to spray the silicone baking mat with no stick spray, but you would need to if you baked directly on the cookie sheet.)

Start by putting handle end of spoon in center of dough and "degas, pull and stretch" dough to form a ball.

Generously dust dough and side of bowl with flour... roll dough in flour to coat. Roll dough (and excess flour) out of bowl onto work surface.

Press lightly to flatten... then divide dough into 8 portions (like a pizza).

Shape portions into rolls by using your fingers to stretch the tops and tuck the dough into the back (add flour as needed to assist with shaping), and arrange in 2 rows of 4 on silicone baking mat.

Place cookie sheet in a warm draft-free location, cover with a lint-free towel, and proof for 30 minutes.

Before dough is fully proofed...

Move rack to middle of oven and pre-heat to 450 degrees F.

30 minutes later

When oven has come to temperature... place cookie sheet in oven and bake for 20 minutes.

20 minutes later

Gently turn rolls out on work surface and place on cooling rack.

Garlic-Herb Rolls (mini round cake pans)
If you like olive oil, garlic and herbs you'll love these rolls. They're easy to make and sure to please. You can use 1/2 tsp each dry Marjoram, Thyme, Basil & Oregano or 2 tsp dry Italian Herb Mix if it's more convenient. And... I used 8 *Wilton* mini round cake pans to shape the rolls.

Garlic-Herb Rolls

Pour warm water in a 3 to 4 qt warm glass mixing bowl (use a warm bowl… you don't want a cold bowl to take the heat out of the warm water).

    14 oz warm Water

Add salt, yeast, herbs, garlic and olive oil… give a quick stir to combine.

    1-1/2 tsp Salt
    1-1/4 tsp Instant Yeast
    1/2 tsp dry Marjoram
    1/2 tsp dry Thyme
    1/2 tsp dry Basil
    1/2 tsp dry Oregano
    1 to 2 tsp Garlic Paste or minced Garlic
    1 Tbsp extra-virgin Olive Oil

Add flour… then cheese… and stir until dough forms a shaggy ball, scrape dry flour from side of bowl, then tumble dough to combine moist flour with dry flour.

    3-1/2 cups Bread Flour
    1/2 cup shredded Parmesan Cheese

Place bowl in a warm draft-free location, cover with a lint-free towel (or plastic wrap), and proof for 1-1/2 hours.

1-1/2 hours later (mini round cake pan)

When dough has risen and developed its gluten structure… spray 8 mini round cake pans (4" x 1-1/4") with no-stick cooking spray, place in rimmed baking sheet (makes it easier to carry them), and set aside.

Start by putting handle end of spoon in center of dough and "degas, pull and stretch" dough to form a ball.

Generously dust dough and side of bowl with flour… roll dough in flour to coat. Roll dough (and excess flour) out of bowl onto work surface.

Press lightly to flatten… then divide dough into 8 portions (as you would a pizza) and place 1 portion in each pan (pan will shape rolls for you).

Place pans in a warm draft-free location, cover with a lint-free towel, and proof for 30 minutes.

Before dough is fully proofed…

Move rack to middle of oven and pre-heat to 450 degrees F.

30 minutes later

When oven has come to temperature… place pans in oven and bake for 20 minutes.

20 minutes later

Gently turn rolls out on work surface and place on cooling rack.

Honey Whole Wheat Rolls (mini round cake pans)
This whole wheat recipe balances the nutrition and nutty taste of whole wheat with the crumb and texture of Country White in a hearty, moist roll with a touch of honey for sweetness. I used 8 *Wilton* mini round cake pans to shape the rolls.

Honey Whole Wheat Rolls

Pour warm water in a 3 to 4 qt warm glass mixing bowl (use a warm bowl... you don't want a cold bowl to take the heat out of the warm water).

    16 oz warm Water

Add salt, yeast, honey and olive oil... give a quick stir to combine.

    1-1/2 tsp Salt
    1-1/4 tsp Instant Yeast
    1 Tbsp extra-virgin Olive Oil
    1 Tbsp Honey

Add flour... stir until dough forms a shaggy ball, scrape dry flour from side of bowl, then tumble dough to combine moist flour with dry flour.

    2 cups Bread Flour
    2 cups Whole Wheat Flour

Place bowl in a warm draft-free location, cover with a lint-free towel (or plastic wrap), and proof for 1-1/2 hours.

1-1/2 hours later (mini round cake pan)

When dough has risen and developed its gluten structure... spray 8 mini round cake pans (4" x 1-1/4") with no-stick cooking spray, place in rimmed baking sheet (makes it easier to carry them), and set aside.

Start by putting handle end of spoon in center of dough and "degas, pull and stretch" dough to form a ball.

Generously dust dough and side of bowl with flour... roll dough in flour to coat.

Roll dough (and excess flour) out of bowl onto work surface.

Press lightly to flatten... then divide dough into 8 portions (as you would a pizza) and place 1 portion in each pan (pan will shape rolls for you).

Place pans in a warm draft-free location, cover with a lint-free towel, and proof for 30 minutes.

Before dough is fully proofed...

Move rack to middle of oven and pre-heat to 450 degrees F.

30 minutes later

When oven has come to temperature... place pans in oven and bake for 20 minutes.

20 minutes later

Gently turn rolls out on work surface and place on cooling rack.

Harvest 8 Grain Whole Wheat Rolls (baguette pans)

These Harvest 8 Grain Wheat Rolls have a more robust and complex flavor than the Multigrain Country White and Wheat Rolls. I experimented with and tested a number of my own multigrain mixtures before I discovered King Arthurs' Harvest Grains Blend and—as they state on their website—the whole oat berries, millet, rye flakes and wheat flakes enhance texture and the flax, poppy, sesame, and sunflower seeds add crunch and great, nutty flavor. Wow... and it's a lot easier and more practical to purchase a blend of seeds.

Generally speaking... I try not to be brand specific, but I did not want to give my readers a list of 8 grains to buy (it would be cost prohibitive). You may want to experiment with a few blends that are available in your community or make your own... it's part of the fun of being your own baker.

And... I used 2 *Matfer* 311141 double loaf French bread pan (18"x 2") to shape these rolls because it has a smooth baking surface. I used to use a perforated baguette pan, but I had too much trouble with the dough sticking in the perforations.

Harvest 8 Grain Whole Wheat Rolls

Pour warm water in a 3 to 4 qt warm glass mixing bowl (use a warm bowl… you don't want a cold bowl to take the heat out of the warm water).

>   16 oz warm Water

Add salt, yeast, sugar, grains, and olive oil… give a quick stir to combine.

>   1-1/2 tsp Salt
>   1-1/4 tsp Instant Yeast
>   1 Tbsp Sugar
>   2/3 cup King Arthur Harvest Grains Blend
>   1 Tbsp extra-virgin Olive Oil

Add flour… stir until dough forms a shaggy ball, scrape dry flour from side of bowl, then tumble dough to combine moist flour with dry flour.

>   2 cups Bread Flour
>   2 cups Whole Wheat Flour

Place bowl in a warm draft-free location, cover with a lint-free towel (or plastic wrap), and proof for 1-1/2 hours.

1-1/2 hours later (baguette pan)

When dough has risen and developed its gluten structure… spray baguette pans with no-stick cooking spray and set aside.

Start by putting handle end of spoon in center of dough and "degas, pull and stretch" dough to form a ball.

Generously dust dough and side of bowl with flour… roll dough in flour to coat.

Roll dough (and excess flour) out of bowl onto work surface.

Press lightly to flatten… and divide dough into 6 portions (as you would a pizza).

Then (one portion at a time)… roll dough on work surface in flour to shape (adding flour as needed) and place in pan.

Place pans in a warm draft-free location, cover with a lint-free towel, and proof for 30 minutes.

Before dough is fully proofed…

Move rack to middle of oven and pre-heat to 450 degrees F.

30 minutes later

When oven has come to temperature… place baguette pans in oven and bake for 20 minutes.

20 minutes later

Gently turn rolls out on work surface and place on cooling rack.

Mediterranean Olive Signature Rolls (mini round cake pans)
These rolls will blow your socks off. You won't be able to find anything like them on the shelf and they're remarkably easy to make. This recipe uses a blend of olives, olive oil, thyme and lemon zest and has a wow factor of 10. I used 8 *Wilton* mini round cake pans to shape the rolls.

Mediterranean Olive Signature Rolls

Prepare flavor ingredients... zest lemon, slice green olives in half, slice kalamata olives in thirds, and set aside.

> Zest of 1 Lemon
> 2-1/4 oz (1 can) sliced Black Olives
> 1 can stuffed Green Olives (use black olive can to measure)
> 1 can Pitted Kalamata Olives (use black olive can to measure)

Pour warm water in a 3 to 4 qt warm glass mixing bowl (use a warm bowl... you don't want a cold bowl to take the heat out of the warm water).

> 12 oz warm Water

Add salt, yeast, thyme, and olive oil... give a quick stir to combine.

> 1-1/2 tsp Salt
> 1-1/4 tsp Instant Yeast
> 1 tsp dried Thyme
> 1 Tbsp extra-virgin Olive Oil

Add flour... then flavor ingredients. Stir until dough forms a shaggy ball, scrape dry flour from side of bowl, then tumble dough to combine moist flour with dry flour.

> 3-1/2 cups Bread Flour

Place bowl in a warm draft-free location, cover with a lint-free towel (or plastic wrap), and proof for 1-1/2 hours.

1-1/2 hours later (mini round cake pan)

When dough has risen and developed its gluten structure... spray 8 mini round cake pans (4" x 1-1/4") with no-stick cooking spray, place in rimmed baking sheet (makes it easier to carry them), and set aside.

Start by putting handle end of spoon in center of dough and "degas, pull and stretch" dough to form a ball.

Generously dust dough and side of bowl with flour... roll dough in flour to coat.

Roll dough (and excess flour) out of bowl onto work surface.

Press lightly to flatten... then divide dough into 8 portions (as you would a pizza) and place 1 portion in each pan (pan will shape rolls for you).

Place pans in a warm draft-free location, cover with a lint-free towel, and proof for 30 minutes.

Before dough is fully proofed...

Move rack to middle of oven and pre-heat to 450 degrees F.

30 minutes later

When oven has come to temperature... place pans in oven and bake for 20 minutes.

20 minutes later

Gently turn rolls out on work surface and place on cooling rack.

Cinnamon Raisin Breakfast Rolls (mini round cake pans)
Homemade fresh from the oven cinnamon raisin breakfast rolls are a great way to start your day. You can slice them in half and toast them or nibble on them just as they are... and when our guests stay overnight, my wife wants them to wake up to the aroma of fresh for the oven cinnamon raisin rolls filling the house. I used 8 *Wilton* mini round cake pans to shape the rolls.

Cinnamon Raisin Breakfast Rolls

Pour warm water in a 3 to 4 qt warm glass mixing bowl (use a warm bowl… you don't want a cold bowl to take the heat out of the warm water).

    16 oz warm Water

Add salt, yeast, sugar, and cinnamon… give a quick stir to combine with a flat whisk or fork (it will make it easier to combine the cinnamon).

    1-1/2 tsp Salt
    1-1/4 tsp Instant Yeast
    2 Tbsp Brown Sugar
    1 Tbsp ground Cinnamon

Add flour… then raisins. Stir until dough forms a shaggy ball, scrape dry flour from side of bowl, then tumble dough to combine moist flour with dry flour.

    3-1/2 cups Bread Flour
    1 cup Raisins

Place bowl in a warm draft-free location, cover with a lint-free towel (or plastic wrap), and proof for 1-1/2 hours.

1-1/2 hours later (mini round cake pan)

When dough has risen and developed its gluten structure… spray 8 mini round cake pans (4" x 1-1/4") with no-stick cooking spray, place in rimmed baking sheet (makes it easier to carry them), and set aside.

Start by putting handle end of spoon in center of dough and "degas, pull and stretch" dough to form a ball.

Generously dust dough and side of bowl with flour… roll dough in flour to coat. Roll dough (and excess flour) out of bowl onto work surface.

Press lightly to flatten… then divide dough into 8 portions (as you would a pizza) and place 1 portion in each pan (pan will shape rolls for you).

Place pans in a warm draft-free location, cover with a lint-free towel, and proof for 30 minutes.

Before dough is fully proofed…

Move rack to middle of oven and pre-heat to 450 degrees F.

30 minutes later

When oven has come to temperature… place pans in oven and bake for 20 minutes.

20 minutes later

Gently turn rolls out on work surface and place on cooling rack.

Small Sandwich Rolls (mini loaf pans)
Look at the crumb... these rolls will make any sandwich special and the mini loaf pans made them uniform in shape. I used 8 *Chicago Metallic* non-stick mini loaf pans (5-3/4" x 3-1/4" x 2-1/4") to shape these rolls (they are very reasonably priced and come in a three pack).

Small Sandwich Rolls

Pour warm water in a 3 to 4 qt warm glass mixing bowl (use a warm bowl… you don't want a cold bowl to take the heat out of the warm water).

>> 14 oz warm Water

Add salt and yeast… give a quick stir to combine.

>> 1-1/2 tsp Salt
>> 1-1/4 tsp Instant Yeast

Add flour… stir until dough forms a shaggy ball, scrape dry flour from side of bowl, then tumble dough to combine moist flour with dry flour.

>> 3-1/2 cups Bread Flour

Place bowl in a warm draft-free location, cover with a lint-free towel (or plastic wrap), and proof for 1-1/2 hours.

1-1/2 hours later (mini loaf pans)

When dough has risen and developed its gluten structure… spray 8 mini loaf pans (5-3/4" x 3-1/4" x 2-1/4") with no-stick cooking spray, place in rimmed baking sheet (makes it easier to carry), and set aside.

Start by putting handle end of spoon in center of dough and "degas, pull and stretch" dough to form a ball.

Generously dust dough and side of bowl with flour… roll dough in flour to coat.

Roll dough (and excess flour) out of bowl onto work surface.

Press lightly to flatten… and divide dough into 8 portions (as you would a pizza).

Then (one portion at a time)… roll dough on work surface in flour to shape (adding flour as needed), press to flatten and place in pan (pan will finish shaping rolls for you).

Place pans in a warm draft-free location, cover with a lint-free towel, and proof for 30 minutes.

Before dough is fully proofed…

Move rack to middle of oven and pre-heat to 450 degrees F.

30 minutes later

When oven has come to temperature… place loaf pan in oven and bake for 20 minutes.

20 minutes later

Gently turn rolls out on work surface and place on cooling rack.

Large Sandwich Rolls (baguette pans)

For long narrow rolls I use baguette pans. In this case, I used 2 *Matfer* 311141 double loaf French bread pan (18"x 2") to shape these rolls because it has a smooth baking surface. I used to use a perforated baguette pan, but I had too much trouble with the dough sticking in the perforations.

Large Sandwich Rolls

Pour warm water in a 3 to 4 qt warm glass mixing bowl (use a warm bowl... you don't want a cold bowl to take the heat out of the warm water).

<u>14 oz warm Water</u>

Add salt and yeast... give a quick stir to combine.

<u>1-1/2 tsp Salt</u>
<u>1-1/4 tsp Instant Yeast</u>

Add flour... stir until dough forms a shaggy ball, scrape dry flour from side of bowl, then tumble dough to combine moist flour with dry flour.

<u>3-1/2 cups Bread Flour</u>

Place bowl in a warm draft-free location, cover with a lint-free towel (or plastic wrap), and proof for 1-1/2 hours.

1-1/2 hours later (baguette pan)

When dough has risen and developed its gluten structure... spray baguette pans with no-stick spray and set aside.

Start by putting handle end of spoon in center of dough and "degas, pull and stretch" dough to form a ball.

Generously dust dough and side of bowl with flour... roll dough in flour to coat.

Roll dough (and excess flour) out of bowl onto work surface.

Press lightly to flatten... and divide dough into 6 portions (as you would a pizza). Then (one portion at a time)... roll dough on work surface in flour to shape (adding flour as needed)and place in pan.

Place pans in a warm draft-free location, cover with a lint-free towel, and proof for 30 minutes.

Before dough is fully proofed...

Move rack to middle of oven and pre-heat to 450 degrees F.

30 minutes later

When oven has come to temperature... place baguette pan in oven and bake for 20 minutes.

20 minutes later

Gently turn rolls out on work surface and place on cooling rack.

Torpedo Sandwich Rolls (baguette pans)

A torpedo is a long thin sandwich loaded with flavor. We like to layer a fresh from the oven torpedo sandwich roll with an assortment of Italian meats, a slice of provolone cheese, then diced tomatoes, shredded lettuce, then finish with salt, pepper, a little oregano... and a drizzle of olive oil. They're smart... they're easy... they're delicious.

And... I used 2 *Matfer* 311141 double loaf French bread pan (18"x 2") to shape these rolls because it has a smooth baking surface. I used to use a perforated baguette pan, but I had too much trouble with the dough sticking in the perforations.

Torpedo Sandwich Rolls

Pour warm water in a 3 to 4 qt warm glass mixing bowl (use a warm bowl... you don't want a cold bowl to take the heat out of the warm water).

    <u>14 oz warm Water</u>

Add salt and yeast... give a quick stir to combine.

    <u>1-1/2 tsp Salt</u>
    <u>1-1/4 tsp Instant Yeast</u>

Add flour... stir until dough forms a shaggy ball, scrape dry flour from side of bowl, then tumble dough to combine moist flour with dry flour.

    <u>3-1/2 cups Bread Flour</u>

Place bowl in a warm draft-free location, cover with a lint-free towel (or plastic wrap), and proof for 1-1/2 hours.

1-1/2 hours later (baguette pan)

When dough has risen and developed its gluten structure... spray baguette pans with no-stick spray and set aside.

Start by putting handle end of spoon in center of dough and "degas, pull and stretch" dough to form a ball.

Generously dust dough and side of bowl with flour... roll dough in flour to coat.

Roll dough (and excess flour) out of bowl onto work surface.

Press lightly to flatten... and divide dough into 4 portions.

Then (one portion at a time) roll dough on work surface in flour to shape and stretch into 14" lengths and place in pan. (When shaping, I find holding the dough over the work surface and allowing gravity to stretch helps with the process.)

Place pans in a warm draft-free location, cover with a lint-free towel, and proof for 30 minutes.

Before dough is fully proofed...

Move rack to middle of oven and pre-heat to 450 degrees F.

30 minutes later

When oven has come to temperature... place pans in oven and bake for 15 minutes.

15 minutes later

Gently turn baguettes out on work surface and place on cooling rack.

Hamburger Buns (mini round cake pans)
I frequently use store bought hamburger buns, but there are times when I'm looking for something special and a fresh from the oven artisan bun can change a good hamburger into a great dining experience. You'll never find a hamburger bun like these in a grocery store. I used 8 *Wilton* mini round cake pans to shape the rolls.

Hamburger Buns

Pour warm water in a 3 to 4 qt warm glass mixing bowl (use a warm bowl... you don't want a cold bowl to take the heat out of the warm water).

    14 oz warm Water

Add salt and yeast... give a quick stir to combine.

    1-1/2 tsp Salt
    1-1/4 tsp Instant Yeast

Add flour... stir until dough forms a shaggy ball, scrape dry flour from side of bowl, then tumble dough to combine moist flour with dry flour.

    3-1/2 cups Bread Flour

Place bowl in a warm draft-free location, cover with a lint-free towel (or plastic wrap), and proof for 1-1/2 hours.

1-1/2 hours later (mini round cake pan)

When dough has risen and developed its gluten structure... spray 8 mini round cake pans (4" x 1-1/4") with no-stick cooking spray, place in rimmed baking sheet (makes it easier to carry them), and set aside.

Start by putting handle end of spoon in center of dough and "degas, pull and stretch" dough to form a ball.

Generously dust dough and side of bowl with flour... roll dough in flour to coat.

Roll dough (and excess flour) out of bowl onto work surface.

Press lightly to flatten... then divide dough into 8 portions (as you would a pizza) and place 1 portion in each pan (pan will shape rolls for you).

Place pans in a warm draft-free location, cover with a lint-free towel, and proof for 30 minutes.

Before dough is fully proofed...

Move rack to middle of oven and pre-heat to 450 degrees F.

30 minutes later

When oven has come to temperature... place pans in oven and bake for 20 minutes.

20 minutes later

Gently turn rolls out on work surface and place on cooling rack.

No-Knead Pizza Dough & Pizza

You'll be pleasantly surprised with how easy it is to make pizza dough. Just mix... wait... and poof, you have pizza dough. And, once you have pizza dough you can make pizzas, calzones, breadsticks, garlic knots or anything else your little ole' heart desires.

"You better cut the pizza in four pieces because I'm not hungry enough to eat six."

Yogi Berra, Baseball Hall of Fame catcher

No-Knead Pizza Dough

I experimented with a variety of herbs, spices, and pizza dough flavor packs, but I found I preferred to add flavors to the pizza toppings versus in the dough, because the flavors I want in a vegetarian pizza are different than the flavors I add to a pepperoni pizza. And I don't use sugar, but it's okay if it's your preference.

I have 2 methods for making pizza dough, "Traditional"… proof for 8 to 24 hours, and "Turbo"… proof for 1-1/2 hours. And, I also have a whole wheat version using the "Turbo" method.

"Traditional" No-Knead Pizza Dough… proof for 8 to 24 hours

The "traditional" method for making no-knead bread is very popular. The same process can be used to make pizza dough.

Pour water into a 3 to 4 qt glass mixing bowl.
> 12 oz cool Water

Add salt, yeast, and olive oil… give a quick stir to combine.
> 1-1/2 tsp Salt
> 1/4 tsp Instant Yeast
> 1 Tbsp extra-virgin Olive Oil

Add flour… stir until dough forms a shaggy ball, scrape dry flour from side of bowl, then tumble dough to combine moist flour with dry flour.
> 3 cups Bread Flour

Cover bowl with plastic wrap, place in a warm draft-free location, and proof for 8 to 24 hours.

8 to 24 hours later

When dough has risen and developed its gluten structure…

Start by putting handle end of spoon in center of dough and "degas, pull and stretch" dough to form a ball.

Generously dust dough and side of bowl with flour… roll dough in flour to coat.

Roll dough (and excess flour) out of bowl onto work surface.

Press lightly to flatten… divide dough into 2 portions and form each portion into a ball.

If you aren't ready to use the pizza dough balls… cover with a lint-free towel to rest.

Congratulations… you have 2 pizza dough balls.

Notes: Pizza dough (like all other flatbreads) doesn't need a 2nd proofing… it can be used immediately. If you wish to save one pizza dough ball… put it in a glass bowl, drizzle with olive oil, roll to coat, cover with plastic wrap and refrigerate for a day or two.

YouTube video in support of recipe: World's Easiest No-Knead Bread (Introducing "Hands-Free" Technique) which demonstrates "traditional" method and "hands-free" technique for making bread dough… the ingredients are slightly different, but the process for making the dough is the same.

No-Knead "Turbo" Pizza Dough… proof for 1-1/2 hours
If you don't want to wait 8 to 24 hours… this is an excellent alterative.

Pour warm water in a 3 to 4 qt warm glass mixing bowl (use a warm bowl… you don't want a cold bowl to take the heat out of the warm water).
> 14 oz warm Water

Add salt, yeast, and olive oil… give a quick stir to combine.
> 1-1/2 tsp Salt
> 1-1/4 tsp Instant Yeast
> 1 Tbsp extra-virgin Olive Oil

Add flour… stir until dough forms a shaggy ball, scrape dry flour from side of bowl, then tumble dough to combine moist flour with dry flour.
> 3-1/2 cups Bread Flour

Place bowl in a warm draft-free location, cover with a lint-free towel (or plastic wrap), and proof for 1-1/2 hours.

1-1/2 hours later
When dough has risen and developed its gluten structure…
Start by putting handle end of spoon in center of dough and "degas, pull and stretch" dough to form a ball.
Generously dust dough and side of bowl with flour… roll dough in flour to coat.
Roll dough (and excess flour) out of bowl onto work surface.
Press lightly to flatten… divide dough into 2 portions and form each portion into a ball.
If you aren't ready to use the pizza dough balls… cover with a lint-free towel to rest.

Poof… you have 2 pizza dough balls in less than 2 hours with only 5 minutes work.

Notes: Likewise, "Turbo" dough can be refrigerated for a day or two.

YouTube video in support of recipe: World's Easiest Pizza Dough… ready to bake in less than 2 hours (no-knead "hands-free" technique)… demonstrates "Turbo" method including "hands-free" technique.

Mushroom-Black Olive Pizza

Prep: Move rack to the middle of oven and preheat to 450 degrees F.
Shape: Place dough in the center of work space, press firmly to flatten… then work from the center pushing the dough outward to make a larger disk adding flour as needed.

> 1 Pizza Dough Ball

Pick disk up by the edge and move your hands along the edge allowing gravity to stretch the dough until it forms a larger circle… then use a pizza roller to finish shaping and place in pizza pan.
Toppings: Spread a thin layer of sauce on the dough, generously sprinkle with cheese, cover with mushrooms, add black olives, and sprinkle with a little more cheese.

> 3 heaping Tbsp Pizza Sauce
> 8 oz shredded Provolone-Mozzarella Cheese
> 6 oz sliced Mushrooms
> 1/2 cup (2-1/4 oz can) sliced Black Olives

Bake: Put pan in oven and bake for 15 to 18 minutes depending on the thickness of the crust, the toppings, and how you like your cheese.
Serve: Remove from oven, slice and serve.

Pepperoni Pizza
Prep: Move rack to the middle of oven and preheat to 450 degrees F.
Shape: Place dough in the center of work space, press firmly to flatten… then work from the center pushing the dough outward to make a larger disk adding flour as needed.
     1 Pizza Dough Ball
Pick disk up by the edge and move your hands along the edge allowing gravity to stretch the dough until it forms a larger circle… then use a pizza roller to finish shaping and place in pizza pan.
Toppings: Spread a thin layer of sauce on dough, generously sprinkle with cheese, and cover with pepperoni (I didn't add a second layer of cheese because pepperoni pizza looks better if you don't cover the meat).
     3 heaping Tbsp Pizza Sauce
     8 oz shredded Provolone-Mozzarella Cheese
     Sliced Pepperoni
Bake: Put pan in oven and bake for 15 to 18 minutes depending on the thickness of the crust, the toppings, and how you like your cheese.
Serve: Remove from oven, slice and serve.

Whole Wheat Cheese Pizza

Prep: Move rack to the middle of oven and preheat to 450 degrees F.

Shape: Place dough in the center of work space, press firmly to flatten… then work from the center pushing the dough outward to make a larger disk adding flour as needed.

<u>1 Whole Wheat Pizza Dough Ball</u>

Pick disk up by the edge and move your hands along the edge allowing gravity to stretch the dough until it forms a larger circle… then use a pizza roller to finish shaping and place in pizza pan.

Toppings: Spread a thin layer of sauce on dough and generously cover with cheese.

<u>3 heaping Tbsp Pizza Sauce</u>
<u>10 oz shredded Provolone-Mozzarella Cheese</u>
<u>2 oz shredded Cheddar Cheese</u>

Bake: Put pan in oven and bake for 15 to 18 minutes depending on the thickness of the crust, the toppings, and how you like your cheese.

Serve: Remove from oven, slice and serve.

Meatball & Bacon Pizza
Prep: Move rack to the middle of oven and preheat to 450 degrees F.
Meatballs... place meatballs on a paper plate, microwave on high for 1 minute, cut in half and set aside.
  12 sm frozen Meatballs
Bacon... trim off excess fat (not all), put paper towel on a paper plate, place bacon in a single layer on one side of the paper towel, fold other side over to cover (prevents splattering), and heat in the microwave on high for 1 to 2 minutes to render the fat, but don't overcook... it's going to be baked.
  4 slices Bacon
Take bacon out of the microwave, remove paper towel, and allow bacon to cool... then cut bacon into pieces and set aside.
Shape: Place dough in the center of work space, press firmly to flatten... then work from the center pushing the dough outward to make a larger disk adding flour as needed.
  1 Pizza Dough Ball
Pick disk up by the edge and move your hands along the edge allowing gravity to stretch the dough until it forms a larger circle... then use a pizza roller to finish shaping and place in pizza pan.
Toppings: Spread a thin layer of sauce on dough, generously sprinkle with cheese, and add bacon and meatballs.
  3 heaping Tbsp Pizza Sauce
  8 oz shredded Provolone-Mozzarella Cheese
Bake: Put pan in oven and bake for 15 to 18 minutes depending on the thickness of the crust, the toppings, and how you like your cheese.
Serve: Remove from oven, slice and serve.

Note: All meat should be precooked before being added to a pizza.

Garlic Breadsticks & Nuggets
Prep: Move rack to the middle of oven and preheat to 450 degrees F.
Shape: Place a silicone baking mat on the work surface and place dough in center of mat.
   1 Pizza Dough Ball
Then press lightly to flatten, drizzle with olive oil, and use a pizza roller to spread the oil and form a small circle, turn dough over, drizzle 2nd side with oil, and use roller (or rolling pin) to shape the dough into a 9" x 12" rectangle 1/4" thick.
   1 tsp extra-virgin Olive Oil per side
Toppings: Add a dab of garlic paste and spread with kitchen knife.
   2 tsp Garlic Paste
Generously brush with melted butter.
   2 Tbsp melted Butter
Sprinkle with cheese.
   Shredded Parmesan Cheese
Use a pizza cutter to cut dough into sticks. Then cut the irregular ends and edges into nuggets.
Bake: Slide cookie sheet under silicone baking mat, place dough (cookie sheet and all) into the oven and bake for 12 to 15 minutes depending on how you like your cheese.
Serve: Remove from oven, slice and serve.

Sweet Rolls

Sweet rolls are the quintessential American breakfast treat that isn't just for breakfast, but remember... "Never eat more than you can lift" (Miss Piggy, Muppet extraordinaire).

No-Knead "Turbo" Sweet Roll Dough

Whether its cinnamon rolls, cinnamon knots, raspberry sweet roll knots, caramel-pecan sweet rolls, or any other sweet roll recipe… the dough remains the same… the process for making the rolls changes.

No-Knead "Turbo" Sweet Roll Dough

Pour milk and melted butter into a 3 to 4 qt glass mixing bowl and microwave on high for 1-1/2 minutes.

- 11 oz Whole Milk
- 4 Tbsp melted Butter

Add salt, yeast, sugar, egg yolk, vanilla extract… and whip to combine.

- 1-1/2 tsp Salt
- 1-1/4 tsp Instant Yeast
- 3 Tbsp Sugar
- 1 lg Egg Yolk
- 1-1/2 tsp Vanilla Extract

Add flour… stir until dough forms a shaggy ball, scrape dry flour from side of bowl, then tumble dough to combine moist flour with dry flour.

- 3 cups Bread Flour

Place bowl in a warm draft-free location, cover with a lint-free towel, and proof for 2-1/2 hours (sweet roll dough needs a longer proofing time).

2-1/2 hours later

When dough has risen and developed its gluten structure... place handle end of spoon in center of dough and "degas, pull and stretch" dough to form a ball. Generously dust dough and side of bowl with flour… roll dough in flour to coat. Roll dough out of bowl (excess flour and all) onto work surface.

Poof... you have sweet roll dough.

Videos in Support of Recipes: No-Knead "Turbo" Cinnamon Rolls… ready to bake in 2-1/2 hours ("hands-free" technique to make dough) and How to Proof Bread Dough (a.k.a. The Dynamics of Proofing).

Old-Fashioned Cinnamon Rolls (Pan Method)
The 9" round cake pan is the perfect baking vessel for cinnamon rolls. It will give you nice thick rolls and everyone can fight over the center roll.

Prep
Make cinnamon-sugar mixture... put sugar in bowl, add cinnamon, stir to combine, and set aside.
>1/3 cup White Sugar
>1 rounded tsp Cinnamon

Spray a 9" round cake pan with no-stick cooking spray and set aside.

Make rolls
Lightly dust work surface with flour and roll dough (excess flour and all) out of bowl onto work surface.
>1 Sweet Roll Dough Ball

Press lightly to flatten... then use a rolling pin to roll dough into a long narrow strip. Dust with flour... then turn dough over (flour will help prevent dough from sticking) and continue to roll into a long strip 8" to 12" wide and as long as possible (thin dough will give you more swirls).
Sprinkle dough with cinnamon-sugar mixture and spread with your hand.
Roll dough up tightly into a log.
Cut dough into 8 sections and place in pan. (I cut the dough in half, then divide each half into four equal section. As I cut each section, I use a plastic bowl scraper to assist in arranging the rolls in the pan.)

Place rolls in a warm draft-free location, cover with a lint-free towel, and proof for 30 minutes.

Prep
Before dough is fully proofed... move rack to middle of oven and pre-heat to 350 degrees F.

30 minutes later
When oven has come to temperature... bake rolls at 350 degrees F for 35 minutes.

While rolls are baking... make glaze
Put powder sugar in medium size bowl, add 2 Tbsp milk, and use a small spatula to combine.
> 2 cups Powder Sugar
> 3 to 4 Tbsp Whole Milk

Stir until glaze begins to come together, then add 1 more Tbsp milk and continue to stir (it should be close to the correct consistency).

Continue adding milk in very small portions until glaze is thin enough to spread, but not runny. (If the glaze sits a little too long and thickens... add a little more milk and stir to thin.)

35 minutes later
Take rolls out of the oven and set aside to cool for 10 minutes.
Then use the spatula to spread 1/2 of the glaze over the rolls while they are still warm.
To serve rolls... remove roll from pan, place on a plate, drizzle with a little glaze (optional), and serve while still warm.

Notes: I use a standard 9" round cake pan for these rolls. If you use a 9" x 12" baking pan... line the rolls up in 2 rows of 4 and reduce the baking time to 30 minutes because the rolls will be wider and thinner.

Old-Fashioned Cinnamon Rolls (Individual Roll Method)
Individual rolls have a nice appearance and are easy to serve.

Prep
Make cinnamon-sugar mixture... put sugar in bowl, add cinnamon, stir to combine, and set aside.
>1/3 cup White Sugar
>1 rounded tsp Cinnamon

Place a silicone mat (or 16" x 12" sheet of parchment paper) on cookie sheet and set aside.

Make rolls
Lightly dust work surface with flour and roll dough (excess flour and all) out of bowl onto work surface.
>1 Sweet Roll Dough Ball

Press lightly to flatten... then use a rolling pin to roll dough into a long narrow strip. Dust with flour... then turn dough over (flour will help prevent dough from sticking) and continue to roll into a long strip 8" to 12" wide and as long as possible (thin dough will give you more swirls).

Sprinkle dough with cinnamon-sugar mixture and spread with your hand.

Roll dough up tightly into a log.

Cut dough into 8 sections and place on cookie sheet. (I cut the dough in half, then divide each half into four equal section. As I cut each section, I use a plastic bowl scraper to assist in arranging the rolls in the pan.)

Place rolls in a warm draft-free location, cover with a lint-free towel, and proof for 30 minutes.

Prep
Before dough is fully proofed... move rack to middle of oven and pre-heat to 350 degrees F.

30 minutes later
When oven has come to temperature... bake rolls at 350 degrees F for 30 minutes.

While rolls are baking... make glaze
Put powder sugar in medium size bowl, add 1 Tbsp milk, and use a small spatula to combine.
>	1 cup Powder Sugar
>	1-1/2 to 2 Tbsp Whole Milk

Stir until glaze begins to come together, then add 1/2 Tbsp milk and continue to stir (it should be close to the correct consistency).

Continue adding milk in very small portions until glaze is thin enough to spread, but not runny. (If the glaze sits a little too long and thickens... add a little more milk and stir to thin.)

30 minutes later
Take rolls out of the oven and set aside to cool for 10 minutes.

Then use the spatula to spread the glaze over the rolls and serve while still warm.

Notes: I like to use a silicone mat (or parchment paper) on a cookie sheet to bake these rolls. The cookie sheet makes it easy to carry the rolls to and from the oven and silicone mat makes it easy to remove the rolls after baking.

Raspberry Sweet Rolls
The raspberry filling gives sweet rolls a delicious refreshing taste.

Prep
Open raspberry pastry filling can and set aside.
> 12 oz (1 can) Raspberry Cake & Pastry Filling

Spray a 9" round cake pan with no-stick cooking spray and set aside.

Make rolls
Lightly dust work surface with flour and roll dough (excess flour and all) out of bowl onto work surface.
> 1 Sweet Roll Dough Ball

Press lightly to flatten… then use a rolling pin to roll dough into a long narrow strip. Dust with flour… then turn dough over (flour will help prevent dough from sticking) and continue to roll into a long strip 8" to 12" wide and as long as possible (thin dough will give you more swirls).
Remove pastry filling from can (I hold the can over the dough and use a kitchen knife to stir the filling as I remove it from the can), and spread (I use a small spatula to spread the filling and remove the excess… I use 60 to 70% of the can). Roll dough up tightly into a log.
Cut dough into 8 sections and place in pan. (I cut the dough in half, then divide each half into four equal section. As I cut each section, I use a plastic bowl scraper to assist in arranging the rolls in the pan.)

Place rolls in a warm draft-free location, cover with a lint-free towel, and proof for 30 minutes.

Prep
Before dough is fully proofed... move rack to middle of oven and pre-heat to 350 degrees F.

30 minutes later
When oven has come to temperature... bake rolls at 350 degrees F for 35 minutes.

While rolls are baking... make glaze
Put powder sugar in medium size bowl, add 1 Tbsp milk, and use a small spatula to combine.
> <u>1 cup Powder Sugar</u>
> <u>1-1/2 to 2 Tbsp Whole Milk</u>

Stir until glaze begins to come together, then add 1/2 Tbsp milk and continue to stir (it should be close to the correct consistency).

Continue adding milk in very small portions until glaze is thin enough to spread, but not runny. (If the glaze sits a little too long and thickens... add a little more milk and stir to thin.)

35 minutes later
Take rolls out of the oven and set aside to cool for 10 minutes.
Then use the spatula to drizzle glaze over the rolls while they are still warm.
To serve rolls... remove roll from pan, place on a plate, drizzle with a little glaze (optional), and serve while still warm.

Notes: My wife and I prefer pastry filling (it has a richer flavor), but many others like raspberry preserves. Both are excellent... you should try both to see which you prefer.

Almond Danish
Treat your friends to a fresh-from-the-oven almond Danish. It's easy to shape and can be divided into any size portion for serving.

Prep
Open almond pastry filling can and set aside.
> 12.5 oz (1 can) Almond Cake & Pastry Filling

Make rolls
Place silicon mate on work surface, lightly dust with flour, and roll dough (excess flour and all) out of bowl onto silicone mat.
> 1 Sweet Roll Dough Ball

Press lightly to flatten… then use a rolling pin to roll dough into a small rectangle. Dust with flour, turn dough over (flour will help prevent dough from sticking) and continue to roll into a rectangle until it covers 80 to 90 % of the silicone mat (10" x 14").

Remove pastry filling from can (I hold the can over the dough and use a kitchen knife to stir the filling as I remove it from the can), and spread (I use a small spatula to spread the filling and remove the excess… I use about 80% of the can).

Fold top edge down just past the middle (center) of the dough, then fold the bottom edge up slightly lapping the top edge (the roll will be two layers thick).

Slide a cookie sheet under the silicone mat (it will make it easier to put the rolls into and take them out of the oven) and cover with a flour sack towel to proof.

Place rolls in a warm draft-free location, cover with a lint-free towel, and proof for 30 minutes.

Prep
Before dough is fully proofed… move rack to middle of oven and pre-heat to 350 degrees F.

30 minutes later
When oven has come to temperature... bake rolls at 350 degrees F for 30 minutes.

While rolls are baking... make glaze
Put powder sugar in medium size bowl, add 1 Tbsp milk, and use a small spatula to combine.

      1 cup Powder Sugar
      1-1/2 to 2 Tbsp Whole Milk

Stir until glaze begins to come together, then add 1/2 Tbsp milk and continue to stir (it should be close to the correct consistency).
Continue adding milk in very small portions until glaze is thin enough to spread, but not runny. (If the glaze sits a little too long and thickens... add a little more milk and stir to thin.)

30 minutes later
Take Danish out of the oven and set aside to cool for 10 minutes.
Then use the spatula to spread the glaze over the Danish and garnish with almonds.

      Sliced Almonds to taste

Slice and serve while still warm.

Notes: I found almond cake & pastry filling more convenient and less expensive to use, than making my own. And, I use a silicone mat as a work surface because it's difficult to move the Danish after shaping.

Caramel-Pecan Sweet Rolls (a.k.a. Sticky Buns)

The quintessential American breakfast treat (and my wife's favorite)... that isn't just for breakfast (just ask her). Sweet roll dough topped with caramel and loaded with pecans. It doesn't get any better than this.

Prep

Make cinnamon-sugar mixture... put sugar in bowl, add cinnamon, stir to combine, and set aside.

> 1/3 cup White Sugar
> 1 rounded tsp Cinnamon

Lightly coat 9" x 13" baking pan with butter (I put the melted butter in the pan, then tip it back and forth until butter lightly coats bottom of pan).

> 3 Tbsp melted Butter

Lightly cover bottom of pan with sugar.

> 2/3 cup packed Brown Sugar

Add pecans (I place them in the pan crown side down so that the crown side will be up when the rolls are turned over for serving).

> 2/3 cup Pecan halves

And set pan aside.

Make rolls

Lightly dust work surface with flour and roll dough (excess flour and all) out of bowl onto work surface.

> 1 Sweet Roll Dough Ball

Press lightly to flatten... then use a rolling pin to roll dough into a long narrow strip. Dust with flour... then turn dough over (flour will help prevent dough from sticking) and continue to roll into a long strip 8" to 12" wide and as long as possible (thin dough will give you more swirls).

Sprinkle dough with cinnamon-sugar mixture and spread with your hand.

Roll dough up tightly into a log.

Cut dough into 8 sections and place in pan. (I cut the dough in half, then divide each half into four equal section. As I cut each section, I use a plastic bowl scraper to assist in arranging the rolls in the pan.)

Place rolls in a warm draft-free location, cover with a lint-free towel, and proof for 30 minutes.

Prep

Before dough is fully proofed... move rack to middle of oven and pre-heat to 350 degrees F.

30 minutes later

When oven has come to temperature... bake rolls at 350 degrees F for 30 minutes.

30 minutes later

Take rolls out of the oven and set aside to cool for 10 minutes.

When pan has cool enough to handle (but the rolls are still warm), remove the rolls by placing a plastic cutting board over the top of the pan, and inverting the two together (the rolls should come out of the pan directly onto the cutting board). It's important to face the pan away from you when you turn it over, because the caramel will still be soft and some liquid may leak as you turn the pan over.

Notes: I used a 9" x 13" baking pan (versus a 9" round pan) so that the rolls will be thin with more surface area for the pecans and caramel.